# Two Weeks In A Land Rover

To order additional copies, please contact us.
BookSurge, LLC
www.booksurge.com
1-866-308-6235
orders@booksurge.com

# Two Weeks In A Land Rover
## *On Safari in Tanzania*

Sherry Norman Sybesma

Jessie Pearl Press
2004

# Two Weeks In A Land Rover

Like all great travelers, I have seen more than I remember, and remember more than I have seen.

Benjamin Disraeli

# Moja (1)

The elephant is as big as a large truck. With his head lowered and his ears flapping, he is headed directly for our Land Rover. In a very low but firm voice, our driver Deo says, "Everyone sit down slowly and be very quiet." All four of us obey immediately, fear and weak knees winning over any temptation to try to get one last photo as the huge bull advances. It is a terrifying moment.

The elephant continues toward us until he is nose to nose with our vehicle. I am frozen in fear, thinking he is going to ram us with his tusks. At the last minute he turns to his right and walks away, using his trunk to uproot a small tree that blocks his path. Thus ends the first major wildlife sighting of my Tanzanian safari.

We had arrived at Kilimanjaro airport at 8:00 the previous night, dazed from 20 hours or more of travel. I had used frequent flyer miles for a business class ticket so I was one of the first people through Customs. "Okay," I thought, "this is going well." I stepped over to the luggage carousel and prepared to claim my duffle. Thirty minutes later, I was in a tiny windowless office filling out a claim form for my missing bag.

My job involves a lot of travel and I was used to my luggage not always arriving with me. However, this time I felt like I had to be a good sport about it because I had made a deal with God on the flight over the Atlantic. My plane was four hours late leaving Newark, which meant it was more probable than not that I would miss my connection in Amsterdam. If so, I would have to fly to Frankfurt, then Nairobi and, from there, take a very tiny plane to a small airstrip on the Serengeti. In addition to the hassle and the roundabout route, I would miss the first several days of my safari experience.

When the plane finally went wheels up in Newark, I am ashamed to say I tried to bargain with God. "If I make my connection in Amsterdam," I prayed, "I won't whine if my bag is delayed." Amazingly, my connecting flight had not left when we landed—and we came in just a couple of gates from where it was boarding. I walked through the door just as they were closing it. I later learned the flight had been late pushing back because a passenger was creating a disturbance. The flight could not take off until he was subdued. (He was being deported which is why he wasn't simply removed from the plane.)

On the one hand, I didn't believe God had intervened in something so trifling—but, at the same time, I had made a deal. I never once complained about my missing luggage during the five days it took for me to be reunited with my bag. Fortunately, I had most of my toiletries and a change of clothes in my carryon. People in our group gave me tee shirts and I was able to buy a couple of other things at one of the lodges. The truth is I could have managed fine if my duffle had been lost in space forever. I learned you really don't need many clothes for an African safari.

Late that first night at the airport, however—when I was exhausted from the long flights and a bit anxious about what lay ahead—I felt more than a little discouraged that my trip was getting off to a less than ideal start. My spirits were lifted by the approach of a handsome young man who greeted me with a dazzling smile as he relieved me of my bulging carryon and welcomed me to Tanzania. This was my first introduction to Nickson, who has become like a second son to me. From the moment we met, I felt a special connection between us and my affection for him and his family is one of the things that has drawn me back to Tanzania in the years since.

Once everyone in our group had gotten their luggage—or, in my case, not—we piled for the first time into the four vehicles we would come to know very well over the next two weeks. Our outfitter, Unique Safaris had sent Nickson and the other young men who would be our safari guides to the airport to pick us up and drive us to the hotel where we were to spend our first night in Africa.

It was pitch black outside, with no streetlights or neon store signs to cut through the darkness. Accustomed to a nighttime world ablaze with artificial light, the darkness alone was enough to remind us we were far from home. The dim illumination of the headlights revealed occasional structures, none of which bore any resemblance to the houses and buildings of our everyday lives. The windows did not glow with lamplight or with the flickering images of a television; no porch or yard fixtures lit a welcoming path to the doorways. We passed very few other vehicles, went through no stoplights, saw no billboards.

The lack of lighting was accompanied by an equally unfamiliar silence. There was none of the omnipresent background noise that is our constant companion in the U.S.—no honking horns, blaring boom boxes, ringing cell phones, screeching car alarms, whining sirens, roaring leaf blowers or droning muzak. The way I relaxed into the quiet of the African night made me realize the price exacted on my body and soul by the unrelenting racket that permeates my daily life.

In addition to the darkness and the silence, I was also struck by the smell of the air. It was a lovely evening—soft and cool and heavily laden with the fragrances of flowers, cooking smoke and other scents I did not recognize. It was not the fake clean smell of room sprays and anti-bacterial soaps but a more honest combination of earth and people, animals and growing things.

At the Impala Hotel in Arusha, our trip leader, Ruth, checked us in and gave us our keys. There were several young men and teens in the lobby. None of them had an ounce of extra fat on their frames and some were very thin. As soon as we got our room number, one of them was beside us to ask which bags were ours. I watched in amazement as they hoisted two and three enormous duffels to their shoulders and carried them up several flights of stairs.

My carryon and camera bag were both densely packed so that they weighed more than their relatively small size might suggest. I was glad to relinquish them to the teenager who offered to help me. Ruth told us she would take care of tipping for our entire group—that she would give a lump sum to the management for distribution to all of the staff who served us. However, the young man who carried my things was so courteous—and so obviously hopeful and needy that I felt I had to give him something. When I handed him a U.S. dollar bill, he rewarded me with a 100-watt smile.

My room was simple and comfortable. The fixtures in the bathroom were a most unusual shade of blue but they worked. It might have been better if they hadn't because I forgot and started to brush my teeth with the tap water. (After making the same mistake a couple more times, I take the advice of John, a seasoned traveler in the group, and begin to keep my toothbrush in a glass next to my bed instead of by the sink). It was late and I was exhausted so I collapsed into the narrow single bed. I was so tired I could hardly keep my eyes open but, even so, I felt a twinge of excitement as I pulled the tent of mosquito netting into place around me. Africa! I was in Africa!

My alarm was set for 6 a.m. but I was awakened before it went off by the hauntingly beautiful sound of morning prayers echoing through the city. By 7:00 I was packed and downstairs ready for our breakfast meeting to formally introduce the drivers and to review the itinerary. At Ruth's suggestion we decided to keep a group journal, with each of us being responsible for capturing one day's experiences. Because an important part of "safari etiquette" is to leave no litter in the bush, Ruth handed out small plastic bags containing several squares of toilet paper and instructed us to use them for "bush toilets" She also warned us to give the drivers some advance notice when we needed to stop because they would have to find a safe spot away from predators. At that point, my lack of extra clothing dropped way down on my list of priorities.

Once our luggage was loaded, our first stop this morning was to change money. U.S. dollars, traveler's checks, and even credit cards are fairly widely accepted in Tanzania; however, Ruth told us there are times when we will need shillings. The place the drivers took us was quite small so some of us waited outside for our turn. Young men selling beads, tee shirts, maps, batiks and other souvenir items immediately crowded tightly around us. They were polite and non-threatening but very persistent. When a member of our group said something critical, one of the men replied, "We have to eat. Would you rather we beg?"

Eventually everyone completed their transaction and we got back in the vehicles to begin the drive out of Arusha. Traffic was chaotic. In addition to lots of vehicles bearing the names of safari outfitters, there were numerous vans that seemed to be public conveyances. They all looked to be several decades old and many appeared to be held together with the equivalent of baling wire and spit. The streets were also full of men pulling heavily laden wooden carts or riding bicycles, the handlebars of which often were piled with loads of implausible heights. One rider was somehow balancing a tall stack of plastic bins full of loaves of bread as he pedaled.

In the city, the pedestrians were mostly men, the majority of which were dressed in Western style clothing. We saw a lot of jeans and many garments had the look of hand-me-downs—like they might have come from church mission groups or other charities. Most of the women we saw—both in the city and in the countryside - were wearing kangas, multi-purpose printed fabric rectangles used in East Africa for skirts, blouses, dresses, shawls, head wraps, baby slings and carrying sacks.

Many of the printed tee shirts that Americans acquire and donate to charity in huge numbers had found their way to Tanzania. I spotted Bloomies, Saks, Nike, as well as the names of beers, liquors, sports teams and universities. As we got closer to the fringes of Arusha, we began to see tables and stalls where used Western clothing was for sale.

People were living and working in structures cobbled together of an assortment of materials—including tin, bricks, sticks, planks, mud and plywood. Doors were sometimes pieces of cloth (yet another use for the ubiquitous kanga). We saw goats and chickens and a few very skinny dogs. Dusty, barefoot women with close cropped hair and elegant posture walked along the road balancing large buckets of water or bundles of firewood on their heads.

We observed school children coming and going, the condition of their uniforms seeming to deteriorate as we got farther from the city. Outside of one very poor looking house, a toddler was twirling about in a fancy Western style party dress that appeared to be made of organza while a number of adults in dirty ragged clothes looked on. There was surely a story there but we would never know it. People sat on blankets next to bunches of bananas and other merchandise they were trying to sell. Occasionally, we saw groups of men and women squatting on the ground next to bags and parcels. The driver told us they were waiting for buses.

On the edges of the city, instead of single animals here and there, we began to encounter herds of goats, cows and donkeys. Occasionally, traffic had to stop while they crossed the road. A couple of times, we worried the driver was going to plow into one of the animals but he seemed to know whether they were going to bolt in front of the vehicle or wait for us to pass. The herds were often in the charge of children who could not have been more than 8 or 9 years old. Dressed in worn dusty clothes and usually without shoes, these youngsters looked at us with wide eyes, sometimes giving us a shy smile or a wave.

After a couple of hours we arrived at Lake Manyara National Park, stopping just outside the gates for a picnic. This park, which is tucked under the Great Rift Valley escarpment, is smaller than others on Tanzania's northern safari circuit. Eighty-nine of Manyara's 127 square miles are taken up by the lake, which is so shallow it virtually disappears in the dry season.

As we ate the box lunches the hotel had packed for us, someone noticed movement in the trees overhead. Monkeys! Our first wildlife sighting! Immediately, everyone in the group had a camera in their hands and was snapping like crazy.

"Do you see them?"

"There are more over there."

"This is so cool."

We burned a lot of film in a matter of minutes. At the end of the day, we would laugh at how excited we were over a few vervet monkeys but at the time we had no idea how much better it would get. Besides, it was the first time any of us had ever picnicked under a tree full of monkeys.

Lunch was forgotten. Our safari had officially started and we were ready for more. Our high spirits were dampened somewhat when we drove into the park. Wearing military camouflage fatigues and looking no older than 17 or 18, the guard at the gate was carrying an automatic weapon. Someone in our vehicle reminded us that taking photos of people in uniform is not allowed in Tanzania. We later learn that being a guard in one of the country's national parks can be a dangerous job, especially for those whose duties include protecting the endangered black rhino. We hear stories about armed mercenaries cutting off a black rhino's horns, leaving its body and that of its would be protector behind.

We wound through narrow dirt roads in the park, seeing several animals from a distance. None of Manyara's famous tree climbing lions was spotted but we did see a male with a long mane and a female lying on a log in the distance. The setting had a primordial beauty and even though they were pretty far away, it was still exciting to realize that those were lions—and this wasn't a theme park or a zoo. Their complete lack of interest in us helped to put to rest any concern we might have had that we would be in imminent danger from lions on safari. Every lion we saw on this trip—and we saw a lot of lions—communicated very clearly through its body language that we were at worst a nuisance and at best invisible. The biggest reaction we ever got was a lion that yawned at us, then got up and walked away.

The four vehicles carrying our group of fifteen moved together and apart as each driver tried to be the first to find something major. Deo had driven off on his own when we spotted the lone elephant. We made a turn slightly to the left and there he was, no more than eight vehicle lengths away. Deo came to an immediate stop and he did not get on the radio to tell the other trucks about the sighting as I expected him to do. My guess is he was concerned the noise might disturb the animal. I discover over the next two weeks that the driver guides have an uncanny sense of what the wildlife will and will not tolerate. Elephants have poor eyesight but good hearing. When they hear loud or strange noises coming from sources they can't visually identify, they can become agitated and attack.

The Land Rover's roof hatch was open so the four people in my group took off our shoes and stood on the seats to observe and take photos of our first elephant in the wild. He was not as large as bulls we would see later in the trip but at 25-30 years old, he was big enough to be impressive. The end of his massive muscular trunk was puddled in front of him on the ground. He watched us watching him, occasionally flapping the huge sails that were his ears - something elephants do to dissipate heat. They also do it prior to attacking. (I have never learned to tell the difference between flapping as fanning and flapping as a warning.) After several minutes, he stomped one of his front feet a couple of times and then started moving toward us. This is when Deo issued his quiet but insistent instructions for us to sit down and make no noise.

I was so terrified as the bull was bearing down on us that I was hyperventilating. However, after he has disappeared into the foliage (probably on his way to elephant "happy hour" to tell his buddies he had scared the crap out of a Land Rover full of tourists), Deo explains we had not been in any real danger. It is very common for elephants to come close to noise sources in order to use their senses of smell and hearing to determine if there is a threat. When that happens, if you remain quiet and still, they will move on and leave you alone. (It also helps not to be wearing any scented products such as perfume or deodorant.)

Later in the trip, we are watching several elephant families numbering over 60 individuals cross a river. One group of females and babies comes up from the riverbank at the spot where we are parked. They mill around for a bit and then one of the females lumbers over to our vehicle, extending her trunk around it like we might run our hands around an unfamiliar object in the dark trying to determine what it was. She is so close that her trunk is just inches from the open window where I sit. It is very difficult to be silent and perfectly still when an elephant is that near—at least, it is for me. I guess we pass muster because the elephant returns to her group, which then crosses the road behind us.

Deo assures us we will have no trouble recognizing a truly angry elephant if we ever run into one. He is proven right on a later safari when I am in a vehicle that is the target of a serious elephant charge. A bull is trying to move away from us, but the way the road curves apparently makes him think we are following him. I hear the driver say "Uh oh!" and then he floors the gas pedal just as the elephant bellows and starts running toward us. He doesn't follow us very far—all he wants is for us to get away from him and, when we do that, he settles down. In addition to proving that Deo was right, the experience also teaches me that elephants are capable of impressive speed and that they look even bigger when they are chasing you.

Manyara's varied habitat supports a wide variety of animals. We see giraffe and zebra mingled together beside a lake, vervet monkeys, several troops of baboons, a blue monkey with its long tail and sad face, Cape buffalo, saucer eyed dik-dik and many varieties of birds, including a white browed coucal. We also see more elephants, which—thankfully—take no notice of us. We encounter baboons sifting through huge piles of fresh elephant dung in the road, looking for seeds. As little as 40 per cent of what an elephant eats is digested so the dung is a food source for smaller animals and birds. Nature wastes nothing.

In mid-afternoon, we pass back through the gate, waving goodbye to the teenaged guard and his weapon. We drive through increasing altitude and dropping temperatures to Ngorongoro Crater, a World Heritage site, which is sometimes referred to as the eighth wonder of the world. At a lookout, we pull off to catch our first glimpse of the caldera, a once active volcano that collapsed some two million years ago. Twelve miles across and circled by walls that rise as high as 1600 feet, it is a magnificent sight.

The steep walls are covered by a thick tangle of trees that opens up at the bottom to a flat expansive natural amphitheater. The 102 square mile floor includes grassland, streams, swampland, lakes, forests, and hills. Looking down from the crater's rim, we have a glorious panoramic view that defies description—and photographs. I have no luck capturing the ethereal color and the shimmering light on film. I have returned to Tanzania twice and each time, my first view of the crater has taken my breath away.

As we drive up the steep road to our hotel on the crater rim, we pass Maasai in red robes. They are a striking sight in the dusk, tall and straight as plumb lines, their feet dusty in sandals that look like they are made of recycled tires. We arrive at the Ngorongoro Serena, an eco-friendly lodge designed to blend into its surroundings, just as night falls. Spilling out of the vehicles and into the lobby, we are greeted by hotel staff offering wet cloths and freshly squeezed passion fruit juice.

Getting my key from Ruth, I walk along a covered walkway for what seems like miles to my room, which is rustic but lovely. There are two single beds flanked by nightstands with small lamps. The furnishings also include a straight-backed chair and a wooden desk on which complementary bottled water has been left. A sliding glass door looks over the crater and undoubtedly affords a stunning view in the daylight hours. The bathroom lacks the opulence we expect back in the states (On a later safari, I stay at a hotel in the crater that has a built in hair dryer in the bathroom!) but it is roomy and boasts a large tiled shower. It also has a wall heater above which I will be able to hang my hand laundry to dry. There are small simple throw rugs on the painted concrete floors. A phone is provided - and ashtrays, something I have not seen in a hotel for ages since I always get a non-smoking room. The closet area is open with limited hanging space and several built-in shelves. There is no TV, no clock radio, no mini-bar—but the bathroom is stocked with fresh towels, soap, shampoo and mosquito repellent.

On the way back down the walkway to dinner, I hear a grunt and turn to see a Cape buffalo in a small grassy opening between the buildings; he is less than 15 feet away with only a flimsy railing separating us. At the time, I do not realize how dangerous these animals are so I don't freeze to the spot and start screaming, which I now know might have provoked him to attack. In my ignorance, I react as I would to a fenced bull back in the U.S. "Howdy big fella," I toss over my shoulder as I keep walking.

On my third Tanzanian safari in 2004, we stay at a lodge on the Serengeti where we are cautioned to have one of the armed guards walk us to and from our room after dark because Cape buffalo come up into the grounds at night. We don't take it too seriously until one of our drivers tells us he had been gored at the lodge several years previously. The quick action of the guards saved his life but his story is frightening—and his scars very ugly. I realize I had been an idiot on the previous evening when I had gone back to my room after dinner without a guard. The lodge and grounds were so upscale and beautiful it had been easy to forget this was, after all, the Serengeti and there are no fences to keep out the wildlife.

Dinner in the Ngorongoro lodge restaurant is fabulous (especially the pumpkin ginger soup) but we don't linger. Jet lag, the time change, lack of sleep and the intense experiences of the day have left us worn out and ready for bed. As I turn in, I realize we have been in Africa for only a little more than 24 hours. The time has been so packed with new things and I have been so present in each moment that it is one of the richest, fullest days I had ever had. With that thought, I am asleep.

# Mbili (2)

I have a list of "Lessons I Learned in Africa." It starts with "I am capable of being a morning person." In my "real life" I find it very difficult to get up when the alarm rings. However, I have no trouble rising before dawn on safari. In Ngorongoro, I am the first in our group to arrive for breakfast. The selection includes an abundant buffet of fruits, juices (more of the previous evening's passion fruit, plus guava) and cereals as well as cooked to order hot foods. The coffee is strong and the service is excellent. At the appointed time we assemble in the lobby, which is full of sleepy eyed tourists milling about waiting for their various safaris to get started. Members of my group find seats in one of our four vehicles and we head down into the crater just as light is breaking.

The fog is so thick I do not know how the driver can see the steep, narrow, winding road; fortunately, it is one-way. We pass a Massai walking in the opposite direction. He has pulled his red robe up over his head, giving him a ghostly appearance in the heavy mist. As we near the crater floor, the fog lifts and the landscape is revealed in a soft light that gives everything we see a magical, dreamlike quality. We begin to spot wildlife.

"Oh my gosh—zebra!"

"What is that out there? Wildebeest?"

"They look a lot like bison."

We also see "Tommies"—diminutive Thompson gazelles with their tails switching like windshield wipers set on high speed - Cape buffalo and, as is to be true throughout our safari, an abundance of birds. Tanzania is heaven for a birder. We sight what we think are more Thompson gazelles but the driver tells us it is actually the larger Grant's gazelle. One of our group says the way to tell the difference is to remember the phrase, "Grant's has pants" which refers to the stripes running down the larger animal's rump and rear legs.

Everywhere we go, a part of the crater wall is visible, its rim hidden by heavy clouds that will burn off later in the day. Although we are very close to the Equator, June is the winter season in Tanzania and, like the previous night, the morning is chill. We are glad for our jackets and caps.

There are animals in every direction - big groups, small groups, individuals off by themselves, adults with babies, babies running and playing together. Ngorongoro has the largest concentration of game in Africa and the greatest density of large predators in the world. However, not all of Tanzania's wildlife has a presence in the crater. There are no giraffe and no female or young elephants.

We stop to let long lines of fat zebras— "*Punda Milia*" in Swahili— cross in front of us. We drive through what seems like hundreds more grazing on both sides of the road. If you focus on the stripes when they are standing in a group, you lose sight of their individual outlines and they become one mass of black and white pattern. This is perhaps what nature intended; it makes it difficult for predators to single out a lone animal to attack. The delineation is even more obscured in the dim light of dawn and dusk, the times when predators are most active.

For many years, the purpose of zebra stripes was thought to be a type of camouflage called disruptive coloration. However, it is now believed that another important function of the stripes may be to allow the animals to identify one another. Each zebra's stripe pattern is unique, like human fingerprints. When a mare gives birth, she keeps her foal separate for several days, which is not typical behavior for herd animals. The thought is that this gives the foal a chance to imprint on its mother's stripe pattern.

These are Burchell's or plains zebras, the most common and most plentiful of the three species remaining in Africa. Their shiny coats help to dissipate the intense heat that burns down on their East African habitat. Like other equids such as horses, zebras have long life spans; in captivity they live as long as 40 years.

Attempts to domesticate zebras have been unsuccessful. Among other things, their backs are not strong enough to carry riders or packs. There are three types of zebra groups, the most common being a family consisting of one male and several females with their young. The family usually travels in a single file line with the dominant female in the lead. The order of the rest of the line reflects each mare's position in the hierarchy. Foals share the status of the mother so that the offspring of the dominant female walks directly behind her and ahead of the other adults. The stallion's position varies—if he joins the line, it is not at any particular point and he often walks ahead of, beside or behind the group.

The mother-foal connection is strong in zebras but male foals also develop associations with the stallion. Young males are not sent from the family at any certain age; they leave on their own between the ages of one and four to join a bachelor herd which is the second type of zebra group. The third is a combined herd of several families and/or bachelor groups.

A common zebra bonding behavior is for two animals to stand side-by-side, but facing opposite directions, and groom each other. They rake their teeth down one another's sides against the nap of the hair. This cleans their coats and probably feels wonderful—at least to a zebra. There is a great story about a man who fastened a stiff brush to a long pole and used it to groom a captive zebra who would not let him near her. Over time, he gradually shortened the pole until he was standing right next to the animal. Eventually, the zebra became so used to the ritual that she tried to groom the man back but the force of her teeth was so painful he had to move away.

Zebras are courageous and loyal. There are many tales of individuals and groups coming to the rescue of other zebras. One of my favorites is of a mare and her foal that had lagged behind their herd. A lion, seeing an opportunity, tried to get to the youngster to take it down. The mother fought valiantly, running and kicking with her strong back feet to protect her baby; however, she began to tire and it looked as though the foal was lost.

Just then, the safari group watching the drama unfold heard the thundering hooves of a large group of zebra running at full tilt across the savannah like the cavalry in an old Western. The lion retreated as the zebras surrounded the mare and her foal, escorting them to safety. The zebras that came to the rescue may not have known the two family members they saved were in imminent danger. It is standard behavior for zebras to go in search of members that become separated from the group.

When danger is perceived, zebras form a semicircle facing out with the young and weak protected behind the line of defense. We observe this behavior many times during our morning in Ngorongoro Crater. In this case the possible danger is us—a number of times lines of zebras stand shoulder to shoulder and stare us down as we drive past them. Often a lead mare stops in the middle of the road in front of our Land Rover and stands guard as her family crosses behind her. The entire time, she fixes us with an unwavering gaze that seems to dare us to make a false move.

We see something moving through the herds of zebra; it looks like a tiny flag waving from a stick almost hidden in the tall grass. When the movement reaches an open space, a plump warthog emerges, carrying its tail in an upright position so that the tuft of bristles on the end does indeed resemble a flag. The warthog is a member of the swine family but if that brings to mind cute little Porky Pig of cartoon fame, think again. Warthogs are grayish, with the heavy compact bodies and powerful, relatively short legs of a pig but their snouts are elongated making their heads disproportionately large. They have flat disk shaped noses, unusual tusks that grow in an exaggerated curve and moles under their eyes. The animal is almost hairless except for the tuft at the end of its tail and a mane of long bristles along its spine. There is something about the way the animal looks and moves that shouts "Attitude"—maybe it is that flagpole of a tail. Male warthogs have the tough guy appearance of street fighters and, in fact, they do have violent clashes in which they charge each other straight on. Warthogs love water when it is available, but one of the reasons they are so widely found in Africa is their ability to live without water for months. Like camels, they are able to tolerate high body temperatures, allowing them to conserve moisture in their bodies.

Warthogs are not the only animals we spot with the zebra. The night after I had signed up for the safari several months earlier, I wrote in my journal, "I am going to Africa! For once I shall go to the animals instead of having them come to me in the artificial environments of circuses, zoos and game parks." One of the ways that seeing wildlife in their natural habitat is different from viewing them in captivity is that here the animals are intermingled rather than segregated in separate exhibits. In a single photograph it is possible to capture several types of wildlife—grumpy looking Cape buffalo grazing among wildebeest and zebra, warthogs weaving about through the herds, birds like the crested cattle egret and guinea fowl pecking at the ground while nearby vultures fight over the remains of a lion kill.

Beyond the animals, we spot distant specs of red moving down the crater walls. The driver explains it is Maasai bringing their cattle down to graze and drink, just as they have for centuries. The Maasai are no longer allowed to live within the crater but they do have some rights to bring their animals in during the day. There is concern that even that may be too much for the crater's ecosystems.

The Maasai do not allow their photos to be taken unless they are compensated and some refuse even then. When we negotiate a dollar to photograph a young warrior, there is some confusion about whether that is the price for our whole group or for each person who takes a picture. Over the course of our safari, the reputation the Maasai have for being intelligent and shred is proven out several times.

There is debate about the reason for the distinctive bright red robes worn by the Maasai. One theory is the color allows them to spot each other from a great distance. Since they must roam so far to find grazing and water for their cattle, this is plausible. Another explanation is the color frightens predators. Although this sounds less believable, lions do seem to avoid the Maasai. Because they take such pride in their appearance, I think perhaps the Maasai favor the red robes because they are aware of how handsome they look in them.

Knowing there are restrooms in the crater, we hold off on bush toilets, thinking we will wait to use the more civilized "facilities." Once there, we realize the bush might have been a better choice. The toilets are pits in dirty concrete and the stench is very strong. (Note: The last time I was in Tanzania, significant improvements had been made to many national park toilet facilities, including this one in Ngorongoro.) The first in line warn the rest of us we need to carry in our own toilet paper. There is no running water and Ruth reminds us to use our Purell or other hand sanitizer. Those of us who have left our bottles in the vehicles borrow from others who have theirs with them. ("Anyone need Purell?" becomes a frequent refrain at rest stops and meals throughout the trip. We joke that "eau de Purell" is the official scent of Westerners on safari.)

After several hours of driving around, it feels good to stretch our legs. We visit with members of our group who are riding in the other three vehicles. We ask the drivers questions about what we have seen. There are a number of vervets running around in the area. Although they are very cute little monkeys with their silver gray coats, black and white faces and big round eyes, we now know that they are pests and we have been warned not to feed them or try to touch them. This group is clearly used to humans; they come close to us and do not appear fearful. The doors to one of our vehicles are open. A vervet hops in, seizes a daypack and starts to make off with it. When the owner grabs it, the animal makes a "kek-kek-kek" sound, and for a moment, appears ready to attack. So much for cute little monkeys.

When we are on the move again, a sea of pink appears in the distance. We know we are approaching a lake but why is the water pink? As we draw closer, the solid pink separates into thousands and thousands of flamingos. We see flamingos landing and taking off, flamingos grooming and catching fish, flamingos sparring and courting, flamingos standing and marching about in mini-parades. The air trembles with bird sounds. The huge greater flamingos, ranging in color from white to pale pink and sporting graceful S-shaped necks emit a two note honk similar to that of a goose. From the hordes of smaller, rose pink hued lesser flamingos there is a constant low hum or murmur. Speechless, we alternate between taking photos and staring in awe at the scene.

As our initial shock at the sight begins to fade, we realize there are also hippos in the water—as well as ibis, herons and cranes. Turning, we see zebras behind us. We are at the beginning of our second game drive day and we already have seen an incredible number of animals. None of us had any idea that it would be like this.

We join other safari vehicles at the hippo pool. At first all I see in the water are big rocks, but then one of them moves. I realize I am looking at hippos doing what hippos do much of the time—nothing. Hippos have no sweat glands and rely on mud or water to keep cool. They spend their days in shallow water, emerging at night to follow well-worn paths onto land to graze. Some of these paths seem too steep for the hippo's barrel shaped bulk (Their hide along can weigh as much as 500 pounds!) to manage but the animal is surprisingly agile. They also are able to move quickly on land and there are many accounts of humans being injured or killed because they were between a hippotamus and the water.

Hippos are nothing like the huggable stuffed animals sold as children's toys or featured in cartoons. They are aggressive, dangerous and armed with razor-sharp incisors and canines that function as tusks. The animal's thick tough hide is a crisscross of old and new scars. They are well adapted to an aquatic life—with small ears, eyes and nostrils that sit high on the top of the head, allowing the rest of the massive body to be underwater. By closing their ears and nostrils, adults can remain completely submerged for as long as six minutes.

Hippos are not the only attraction at the pool; the area is teeming with wildlife. There are lions scattered around, herds of zebra and wildebeest close by. A lion on a little rise lifts his head and shakes it, causing what looks like hundreds of previously invisible black and white birds to take to the air briefly, before settling back down into the grass.

We draw close to one of our other vehicles and learn we just missed some excitement. An elephant had suddenly trumpeted and charged some of the lions. The elephant is now disappearing into the distance and the lions have returned to their original spot.

The attraction for the lions is a Cape buffalo that has become stuck up to his belly in some mud. The lions are waiting for him to tire so they can kill him without being gored. Every once in awhile, one of the lions walks down to the buffalo like a cook checking on a turkey in the oven. Each time, the buffalo shakes his head fiercely and the lion goes back to her nap. Our driver tells us the lions will wait for days if necessary.

We feel sorry for the buffalo; we want to get out of our Land Rover and save him. Buying our meat in plastic wrapped Styrofoam trays at fluorescent-lit 24-hour supermarkets has insulated us from the reality that the cow had to be killed for us to have the steak. Intellectually, we know the buffalo must die in order for the lions to live but being part of the story as it plays out makes us uncomfortable. We leave and return later in the day. The buffalo is still stuck; the lions are still waiting.

At noon, the drivers tell us they are going to find a place suitable for today's box lunch picnic. However, there is a surprise in store. When we stop, it is at a grove of yellow-barked acacias surrounding a clearing filled with tables covered in while linen. Staff people from the lodge give us cool cloths to wash our hands and faces before we go through a buffet line featuring *"nyama choma"* or grilled meat. When we take our plates (china, not paper) to the tables, we are offered wine in stemmed glasses or bottles of the Tanzania beer many of us have already come to love—Tusker and Kilimanjaro. It must have taken the staff hours to haul all of this stuff out to the bush so we could dine in style. If I were to look in a mirror and see Meryl Streep staring back at me, I would not be surprised. It feels like I am in her movie.

The lodge workers who are providing our bush lunch are some of the same people who prepared and served our pre-dawn breakfast. When the meal is over and we have gone back to our game drive, they will have to load everything up again, unload it at the lodge, wash it and put it away. Later tonight, they will be the cooks and wait staff at dinner. When we have retired to our rooms, they will still be cleaning up and preparing for tomorrow's breakfast. The hours worked by the average Tanzanian are daunting and the pay is at most a few dollars a day. In spite of this, the quality of service, and the graciousness with which it is offered, are consistently exceptional.

During the afternoon game drive, we see many crowned cranes, the official bird of Uganda. They are beautiful birds, often seen in pairs. Their bodies are blue-gray, white and black, their heads black and white with bright red markings. Set low on the top of their heads is a golden spray of feathers that looks like a headdress. In spite of their plump bodies, they remind me a bit of Las Vegas showgirls in costume. They have that same regal carriage and deliberate gait.

We also see the large secretary bird, it's walk resembling a typist striking keys. Then, incredibly, the drivers spot black rhino in the distance. I am told there are two of them in the middle of a large group of wildebeest but, at first, I have difficulty finding them. Then the distinctive prehistoric shape jumps into view in my binoculars. With fewer than 20 left in Ngorongoro, not all safari groups are fortunate enough to see black rhino. In addition to their scarcity, in amongst the herds of more plentiful animals, they can be hidden in plain sight—as the ones we saw would have been except for the keen trained eyes of our driver guides. During the course of the safari, ours were often the only vehicles present for some amazing wildlife viewing, a testament to the skill and knowledge of our Unique Safari drivers.

The rhinoceros dates back millions of years to the Miocene era but in recent decades the population has been so decimated by poaching that the animal is in danger of becoming extinct. Current rhino numbers are only about 10 per cent of what they were in 1970. Rhinos have no natural predators; predation by men solely for its horns is the only real threat the rhino faces but it is serious one.

A tendency to charge without provocation has added to people's fear of rhinos and to their reputation for being ill tempered. The arbitrary charging is probably the result of poor eyesight. The oxpeckers, or tickbirds, that accompany rhinos everywhere help to compensate for the animal's bad vision by making a noisy ruckus when they sense danger. The Swahili name for the birds is *"askari wa kifaru"* which means "watchman for the rhino".

Rhinos are a verbal species, emitting many different sounds, the most fearsome being the snort the animal makes as it lowers its head to charge. Both white and black rhinos have two horns—although, in fact, they aren't horns at all but rather tight, dense mattes of hair growing out of the skull. The horns are used both to gore their victims and to strike punishing blows. In spite of their awkward looking shape and their weight of as much as two tons, rhinos can turn on a dime—and they can gallop at speeds up to 30 miles per hour.

On my second safari, also with Unique, we watched for an hour as, not too far away, a large male black rhino attempted to court a female with an older calf. The female rhino was undecided about whether to accept the male's advances. She moved toward him or allowed him to move toward her, then retreated over and over again. With black rhinos, it is the female who decides whether mating will take place and the male clearly understood he had to win her favor if he was going to be successful.

The male repeatedly bent to smell places where the female had urinated, each time throwing his head back and pulling his lips away from his teeth in an exaggerated grimace. His agitation was an indication she was in estrus. The calf was confused, perhaps sensing that his mother's consideration of mating again meant the time was nearing for him to leave her protection. Understandably, he seemed intimidated by the huge suitor. It was a fascinating drama with the animals in almost constant motion.

Just as it appeared the female was going to accept the male, a vehicle from another safari outfitter came careening at a high speed down a road on the other side of the rhinos, causing them to disperse. We lamented the irresponsible behavior of the driver but our own guides told us it might not have been entirely his fault. Apparently, some safari clients insist their drivers behave very aggressively if they want tips. Since tips are the primary source of their income, drivers are caught in a difficult position. Driving too fast or too close to the wildlife or into prohibited areas can result in heavy fines or even the loss of your license. Failing to please the client can have a significant negative impact on income. Our drivers like working with our Sierra Club sponsored trip because we are environmentalists and understand a safari is not an animal park with scheduled appearances by the wildlife.

In the heat of the afternoon, we don't see many animals but we enjoy driving through the beautiful scenery. Ruth tells us the yellow barked acacia we pass are also known as "Fever Trees". The name dates back to when early explorers came to Tanzania and camped beside the lakes and streams along which the yellow acacia were growing. Many of them became ill with a fever we now know was malaria. The explorers associated the sickness with the trees, not realizing they were actually becoming ill from mosquito bites.

Park rules say we must be out of the crater by 6:00. We stay till the last possible minute and, just as we are leaving, we pass several female lions with eight cubs, one of them very tiny. Adult lions are unimpressed by the presence of humans but they keep their babies out of sight. In this case, we can't stop to observe and are gone before they have a chance to hide the cubs. The sighting is a thrilling way to end an unforgettable day.

Tonight's dinner is more festive, both because we are rested and because we are getting to know one another. In the past 48 hours, we have shared experiences we will remember for the rest of our lives. Conversation flows easily; there is much to talk about.

Jenna, the youngest member of our group is celebrating her 13th birthday. Her mother Julie has arranged for the hotel to make a cake and, as they present it, the staff sings a celebration song in Swahili, called *"Jambo Bwana"* ("Hello Sir"). It is another delicious meal and I realize it is unlikely I will need the nutrition bars I brought with me in case the food in Africa was inedible.

We discover the gift shop and buy souvenirs and postcards. We mail the latter that night or the next morning but, even so, we are back home before our family and friends receive them. Our laundry is delivered to our rooms and we are astonished at how little we are charged for the service.

The lodge has a computer terminal where we can log on to send and receive email. A couple of people try it but the per minute fee is high and the hook up painfully slow. There also is long distance telephone service but I calculate that it is about five in the morning back home—and my husband is not an early riser.

Unable to completely resist the lure of technology, I pay $10.00 to send a fax to tell the people in my office I have arrived safely but without my luggage—and that I have already experienced my first elephant charge. Getting a fax from Africa will make my colleagues re-think their opinion that I have gone to an uncivilized place—while the comment about the elephant will reinforce the belief that I am on a wild, untamed and dangerous adventure.

By the time I get back to my room and finish packing up to leave tomorrow, it is 11:00—and we are to meet for breakfast at 6 a.m. I can't keep my eyes open to write in my journal so I put it off (again) for another night.

# Tatu (3)

Tonight we sleep under canvas on the Serengeti! I am sitting in front of a campfire using the light from the flames to finish my entry in the group journal before dinner. One of the camp staff is serving warm roasted peanuts and taking our drink orders. I ask for a glass of wine. The fire is toasty but even with my jacket on, my backside is chilly. It is going to be a cold night; we will need the blankets that are on the cots in our tents.

We left Ngorongoro this morning and drove to Olduvai Gorge. Thirty miles long and 295 feet deep, the gorge is often referred to as the "cradle of mankind" because of the important fossil evidence that has been found there.

We sat in a covered area with a commanding view of the gorge while an anthropologist spoke to us about how it has contributed to our knowledge of early hominids. We learned the site was discovered in 1911 by a German entomologist, Professor Kattwinkel, while he was looking for butterflies. When he returned to Europe, he took with him fossils that were determined to be from an extinct three-toed horse. The intent was to call the site *"Oldupai"*, which is the Maasai name for the wild sisal that grows abundantly in the area. Somehow, the Germans got the spelling wrong and it became "Olduvai" for posterity.

A few years after Kattwinkel's discovery of the gorge, a German geologist named Reck led an expedition to Olduvai and brought back additional fossils from the site. The fossils collected by the Germans caught the attention of Kenyan born archeologist Dr. Louis Leakey while he was visiting Berlin. Working with Reck, Leakey made his first expedition to Olduvai in 1931.

Leakey's wife, Dr. Mary Leakey, uncovered the 1.7 million year old skull of "Zinjanthropus" (Nutcracker Man) in 1959. Sixteen years later her discovery of 3.7 million year old fossilized footprints at nearby Laetoli offered the first proof of pre-humans that had walked upright.

We were excited about driving down into the gorge. However, other than a marker commemorating Mary Leakey's discovery, there was really nothing to see. Since we were not archeologists or geologists, we were unable to read the multi-layered stories that were undoubtedly written in the sediment and rocks surrounding us. On the other hand, our knowledge of the history of the place gave significant meaning to just being there. We were aware of being an extension of something that had begun at this spot millions of years ago and that continues through us to our children's children and beyond. On a more practical, less philosophical level, we realized how unlikely it had been for Leakey to find those few small footprints in this vast, hot, dusty expanse.

From Olduvai, we drove to the Serengeti, Tanzania's most famous national park. The name comes from *"Siringet"*, a Maasai word that means "the place where the land goes on forever"—or, more familiarly, "endless plains." However, over half of the park actually is woodland and bush. The rich soil of the grass plains in the southern part of the park is the result of thick layers of ash blown from volcanoes in the Ngorongoro highlands in the distant past before human time began. The Serengeti ecosystem today is much as it was a million years ago and is possibly the most complex and spectacular on the planet.

The man credited with discovering the Serengeti is American hunter Stewart Edward White. In 1913 when great expanses of Africa were unexplored by Caucasians, White left Nairobi and headed south. "We walked for miles over burnt out country", he said. "Then I saw the green trees of the river, walked two miles more and found myself in paradise." He made his excursion under what he called, "the high noble arc of the cloudless African sky." Over 90,000 travelers now visit White's paradise each year.

Tanzania was not yet independent and still called Tanganyika back in 1951 when the Serengeti became the country's first national park. At that time, it included the Ngorongoro Crater. When the boundaries were adjusted in 1959, the crater was made part of the Nogorongoro Conservation area and more land was added to create the Serengeti as we know it today, which is about the size of Connecticut. The park, which makes up approximately half of the Serengeti ecosystem, generates more revenue than it expends; the excess is used to help support other national properties.

Tanzania, the largest of the three East Africa countries (Tanzania, Kenya, Uganda), has won international recognition for its conservation policies. In a recent award ceremony at the International Trade Center in Washington, DC, Dr. Patrick Bergin, President and CEO of the

African Wildlife Foundation referred to Tanzania as a shining example for environmental protection.

Tanzania is the first county to receive the AWF award, which has previously been given to individuals for significant personal contributions to wild life conservation. In presenting the award to Tanzanian president Benjamin Mkapa, Dr. Bergin said, "Since independence in 1961, Tanzania's successive governments have demonstrated strong commitment to ensure the flora and fauna of Tanzania are preserved for the benefit of future generations. This has placed Tanzania in a unique position in terms of wildlife conservation."

The areas set aside for conversation by Tanzania include 12 National Parks, the Ngorongoro Conservation Area, 13 Game Reserves and 38 Game Controlled Areas. These properties constitute 25% of the country's lands. This commitment to conservation is particularly impressive given the poverty in Tanzania. Twenty per cent of the population is estimated to live on as little as $1.00 US per day.

In his 1961 Arusha Manifesto, Tanzania's first president Julius Nyerere said, "The survival of our wildlife is a matter of grave concern to all of us in Africa. These wild creatures amid the wild places they inhabit are not only important as a source of wonder and inspiration, but are an integral part of our natural resources and our future livelihood and well being.

"In accepting the trusteeship of our wildlife we solemnly declare that we will do everything in our power to make sure that our children's grand-children will be able to enjoy this rich and precious inheritance.

"The conservation of wildlife and wild places calls for specialist knowledge, trained manpower and money, and we look to other nations to co-operate with us in this important task—the success or failure of which not only affects the continent of Africa but the rest of the world as well."

Through my visits to the country, I have gotten to know Joseph Kitia, an instructor in wildlife management and a former Tanzanian game warden who now is the elected leader of Usa River, a progressive village on the outskirts of Arusha. One day on my third safari, when we were driving through the Seronera section of the Serengeti, Joseph called my attention to a mountain in the distance. He told me it was called *"Kalima Pesa"* or "Money Mountain" because of the gold mines buried there. In the 1960's, under President Nyerere, the mines had been closed because they were in conflict with the country's conservation priorities.

Joseph also pointed out the golden grasses we were driving through had similar soil requirements to wheat—i.e., the land could have been used for agriculture but it was set aside for wildlife habitat rather than being cultivated. One of the most amazing things about Tanzania is that even the poorest citizens seem to support the country's commitment to conservation. They see the land and its wildlife as things to be preserved and protected.

On my first safari, we entered the Serengeti at the Naabi Hill gate in the southern corner of the park. We had our box lunch of boiled eggs, meat, fruit and bread at concrete tables in a small picnic area at the entrance. As we ate, aggressive superb starlings looking for handouts surrounded us. These birds are so common in Tanzania that the natives take no notice of them. However, they are quite stunning with a black head, iridescent blue-green back feathers, a bright orange belly and a yellow eye. Superb starlings make a number of sounds, including warbling and chattering.

After lunch we had some time to explore while Ruth and the drivers completed paperwork related to our stay in the park. Most of us took a few minutes to view a photo exhibit mounted on the outside rock wall of the small building that houses the offices for the Naabi Hill gate. The photographs and their captions told the story of Dr.Bernhard and Michael Grzimek, a father and son who, with famed wildlife filmmaker Alan Root, made the classic movie, "Serengeti Shall Not Die."

Dr. Bernhard Grzimek came to fame when he took on the challenge of re-building the Frankfurt Zoo after WWII. It was a daunting task; few animals had survived and the facilities were mostly in ruins. Dr. Grzimek enlisted Allied troops stationed in Frankfurt as volunteer labor and enlarged the zoo by acquiring adjacent properties that had been bombed out in the war. Under his leadership, the small Frankfurt Zoological Society was transformed into a powerful conservation organization; today the Society raises funds to support projects across the world.

On collecting trips to Africa, Dr. Grzimek became concerned about the wildlife in the countries he visited. He expressed his concerns in "No Room for Animals", which became a bestseller. His son Michael made the book into a successful movie, with the intention of donating the profits to Tanzania for the purpose of buying additional land to enlarge the Serengeti.

Peter Malloy, who was Director of National Parks for Tanzania at the time, thought a more pressing need was the gathering of baseline data about the migration that could be used to determine meaningful boundaries for the park. He suggested the funds from "No Room for Animals" be used to map the migration movements of the great wildebeest herds. The Grzimeks' response says much about the kind of men they were.

At ages 48 and 23 respectively, Dr. Grzimek and Michael took flying lessons, bought a single engine Dornier (which they painted in zebra stripes) and set off for Africa to personally map the Serengeti's Great Migration.

Michael turned out to be a natural pilot and his skills in combination with the Dornier's sturdy nimbleness were exactly what the challenging project required. Landings were made in hundreds of remote locations where no plane had ever been and hundreds of thousands of moving animals were counted. Some of the techniques were groundbreaking— e.g., immobilizing animals and marking them so they could be tracked.

The flying involved was often dangerous and Michael had some close calls in the Dornier. At the age of 25, his luck ran out when he lost control of the plane and crashed after hitting a vulture above the Gol Mountains east of the Serengeti. He was buried on the rim of Ngorongoro Crater under a headstone that reads, "He gave all he possessed for the wildlife of Africa, including his life."

On the official Serengeti website, Alan Root writes of Michael's father, "Dr. Grzimek had more effect on wildlife conservation in Africa, and especially in Tanzania and the Serengeti, than any other individual. Today his legacy races across those endless plains and roars at the African moon. Everyone who stands in awe at the unfolding spectacle of the Serengeti owes a debt of gratitude for the life and work of Bernhard Grzimek."

That spectacle was about to unfold for us. We moved from the photo exhibit up a short path to a rise that gave us a view out over the Serengeti. I think all of us were having trouble believing we were seeing in person a place we had read about all of our lives, a place of legend and of countless adventure tales. The only thing that kept us from sticking around to admire the view was the knowledge that as soon as we were all back in the vehicles, our own Serengeti adventure would begin.

We made a game drive through the park rather than going directly to our campsite. We saw an abundance of wildlife, including lion, cheetah, leopard, a spitting cobra, crocodile, buffalo, topi, eland, giraffe, warthog, hyena, jackal, a monitor lizard, and elephant. The birds we spotted included secretary birds, kori bustard (one of the world's heaviest flying birds), superb starlings, red-billed buffalo weavers, pin-tailed whydahs, shrikes and auger buzzards.

The bulk of the migration had already passed the area of the park we were in, but we did see stragglers—wildebeest, zebra and gazelle— following the "long and winding road" to Kenya. At one point in the afternoon, we interrupted our game drive to go to a tiny airstrip and pick up Pat, a member of our group who had not made her original flight. Realizing how much she had missed reinforced for me how lucky

I was it had been only my luggage that had missed the connection in Amsterdam.

With our group now numbering 16, we resumed exploring the Serengeti. Almost as interesting as the wildlife were the kopjes (pronounced "copies"), an Afrikaans word meaning "little head." Shaped by the elements over many centuries, these ancient rock formations play critical roles in life on the Serengeti. They provide an environment for plants to grow, they provide shelter for a wide variety of animals and they capture water. Some of them are so beautiful that it would be easy to believe the best landscape designers in the world had painstakingly created them.

There are six main groupings of kopjes on the Serengeti—Barafu, Gol, Maasai, Loliondo, Simba and Moru—and each is distinctive in its own way. The Moru kopjes, the most western in the park, are large and provide homes for an abundance of wildlife. On one Moru kopje there are Maasai paintings at the mouth of a cave that was once used by boys undergoing rites of passage to manhood. After ritual circumcision, the boys would live in the bush for the next several months, spending time in the cave with elders who prepared them to move to the next stage in their lives as Maasai men, that of Morani or warrior. During this period, the boys painted their faces white and wore black robes. The government stopped use of the cave for this purpose about 50 years ago.

Another unique feature in the Moru kopjes is "Gong Rock". One side of this large boulder has many shallow depressions about the diameter of ping-pong balls. Striking the boulder with a small rock creates a bell like sound. In addition to the unusual musical rock, a phenomenal view makes this kopje worth climbing.

On the road below the Gong Rock kopje, I got my first glimpse of a dung beetle. Black with a greenish cast, the insect was rolling a ball of dung larger than she was through the dirt. Her destination was an underground tunnel where she would deposit it with many other balls of dung in each of which she would lay a single egg. The dung would feed the larvae when they hatched and many of the larvae would, in turn, become food for a variety of birds and small animals.

We got to our campsite later than we had intended; it was dusk when we arrived. In the fading light, we saw a line of nine small tents and a larger dining tent. Behind every other sleeping tent were two canvas enclosures, one with a chemical toilet and the other with a "sun shower".

The staff greeted us with juice and the camp manager showed us how to flush the chemical toilets and also told us to be cautious when getting up to go to the toilet in the middle of the night. After hearing that I should not turn and run if I saw a lion but, rather, slowly back away, I decided to cut the top off one of my empty water bottles for as an emergency chamber pot if needed.

Staff members carrying our luggage showed us to our tents. It was too late tonight for showers but the canvas "sinks" suspended from wooden tripods in front of each tent were filled with warm water so we could wash the dust off our hands and faces. We used wet wipes from our luggage to get the worst of the grime off the rest of our bodies. I think the "modern conveniences" I came to value most on the trip were disposable wet wipes, bottled water and zip lock bags.

When I emerged from my tent after changing from shorts to long pants, it was totally dark; lanterns had been lit and hung along the path to the dining tent. They cast a warm golden glow that added to the ambiance of the setting but I still needed my flashlight. My guess is the lanterns were as much to keep wildlife out of the camp as they were to help us see where we were going. It wasn't quite time for dinner so we gathered around the fire and talked about the events of the day. This is where I am now, finishing my entry in the group journal. Beyond our little patch of lanterns and firelight, there is absolute darkness, absolute silence.

How do I describe what it is like to sit in front of a fire on the Serengeti in the deep darkness of an African night? In some ways it is similar to any other camping trip; there is liberation in the absence of all of the choices, options, diversions and distractions that crowd our normal lives. With nothing to do, we don't have to feel guilty for doing nothing.

We are 16 people who would have little in common if we had met back home. There, our jewelry and clothing, our cars and hairstyles, our job titles and bank accounts, our neighborhoods and school districts, would define who we were and where we belonged. Here the familiar pecking order and competition for status and recognition are suspended; in this ancient place we all are beginners and seekers.

We gaze at the flames and let our minds float free. Our thoughts must take similar paths because whenever someone says something, it is almost exactly what I am thinking at that moment—and I sense the same is true for others in the fire circle. Wood smoke and contentment fill the air. I have never been here before and, yet, I feel like I have returned home after a long absence. I think this is the moment when Africa first begins to claim me for her own.

When dinner is called, we go into the dining tent and find it ablaze with candles. We sit around a long table covered with an African print cloth and enjoy a delicious meal, starting with an exquisite soup. It is hard to believe everything has been cooked outdoors over an open fire, especially the fresh bread. Before we adjourn to our tents for the night, one of the Unique Safari owners stops by to greet us. He tells us there is a pride of lions nearby.

We get ready for bed; there is a constant sound of zippers as people go into and come out of the toilet enclosures. It is quite chilly and, without pajamas (they are in my missing duffle), I decide to sleep in my clothes. Staff has added a second blanket to the cot while we were at dinner and when I lay down I pull both over me. As my head hits the pillow, I am overwhelmed by the realization that I am in a tent on the open Serengeti. As I shut my eyes, I say out loud, "This is amazing!" I fall asleep quickly but in the wee hours I am awakened by a throaty, rumbling noise. It is lions roaring on the endless plains.

# Nne (4)

It is still dark at 5:30 the next morning when I hear footsteps and then a splash of water outside my tent as someone fills my canvas sink. "*Jambo*, Miss," a man says softly. "*Jambo*. Time to wake up Miss." I reply, "*Sijambo Bwana. Asante sana.*" ("Greetings, sir. Thank you.") The "*Jambo man*" is one of the things that always comes to mind when I think of camping on the Serengeti. It is a nice way to be awakened.

Stepping from my tent into the dark, I bend my head over the canvas sink and let the warm steam cover my face. The hot water feels wonderful on my hands; it is really cold this morning. Because of the temperature and because I don't have many clothes to choose from, I change my shirt but go to breakfast in the same pants.

It is not yet dawn so the dining tent is once again candlelit. We discover that one luxury we will not enjoy in the bush is brewed coffee. We pour steaming water from a thermos into mugs and stir in spoonfuls of a very finely ground African instant coffee. Perhaps it is the setting— or the early hour—but we are pleasantly surprised at how good the instant coffee tastes. It is deep and rich.

There is a buffet with juice, milk, fruit and porridge. On the table are toast, butter, peanut butter and jam. Assuming this is breakfast, we dig in with the kind of appetite that always seems to accompany a camping trip. Then, the staff person assigned to the dining tent comes in to take our orders for bacon and eggs. Someone asks if anyone else heard the lions roaring during the night. Most of us had but a few are disappointed that they had slept through the excitement. As we eat, the sun rises and when we finish breakfast, we walk out into the beginning of a sparkling new day on the Serengeti.

We spend much of the morning game drive watching a very big pride of lions. We have been observing five or six females for several minutes when someone in another of our vehicles says, "Look—there are more over there." Sure enough there are about four more directly behind us. Then we realize there is a single female lying in the grass off to the left. At this point, we all begin to actively scan the area for more animals. We end up spotting about 17 in all. Our vehicles are completely surrounded by lions! They blend so well with the golden grasses it is sometimes hard to see them even when we know where they are. When they lie down in the tall grass, they become completely invisible. We will remember that later when we stop for a bush toilet. Often on game drives, we sense the presence of animals even though we can't see them.

Several lions are napping under a tree out in the open so that we have a good view. They look like oversized housecats, lying on their backs curled up against one another with their softball-sized paws up in the air. Occasionally one of them wakes up long enough to stretch and yawn before returning to her nap. I am sure if any of us is foolish enough to get out of the vehicle, the lions will notice. However, short of our offering an opportunistic snack, they completely ignore us. Our fascination with their every move is not reciprocated; we do not exist for them.

A highlight of the morning is our first sighting of the lilac-breasted roller. Common in Tanzania, this bird is like a rainbow with wings; it's coloring is spectacular. The *National Audubon Field Guide to African Wildlife* describes the bird's coloration, "Heavy black bill; pale green crown and nape; black line through eye; white eyebrow and chin. Dark purplish-lilac throat and chest with fine white streaks; turquoise belly, wing patch, rump, and tail. Cinnamon-rufous back; dark purple shoulders."

Unlike most birds that have flown away quickly when we stop to observe and take photos, this lilac-breasted roller does not flee the scene immediately. The bare branch on which it is perched shakes in the breeze, ruffling the bird's feathers and requiring it to constantly adjust its balance. It moves his head in typical jerky, bird-like movements, looking up and down and all around. Eventually, it tires of our company and takes to the air, treating us to the sight of all of those lovely colors in motion.

Down the road we see an elephant with two babies, a tiny one suckling and the other—a little older—working on learning to use his trunk. He grabs a hunk of grass and tries to get it to his mouth but the appendage won't cooperate. It twirls around in the air like an out of control garden hose when you let it go with the water running full force. By the time he finally makes it to his mouth, there is almost nothing left. Undaunted, he grabs more grass and tries again.

We see a number of ostriches, including males (roosters) courting females (hens) by dipping low to the ground and shaking one wing at a time to make their loose, shaggy feathers twirl and frill wildly. The giant ostrich does not fly; it uses its feathers only for rituals like shows of dominance/submission and courting. Unlike many birds, ostriches do not have a gland that secretes a waterproof substance. They get soaked when it rains and a drenched ostrich is a pitiful sight.

Fossils date the ostrich back over 120 million years and it is the largest, heaviest bird living today. The often-repeated story about the bird sticking its head in the sand is a myth; it probably grew out of an unusual defensive posture the ostrich adopts when it is in danger and cannot run away. The bird collapses to the ground with its neck stretched straight out flat in front. Because of the neck's light color, it blends with the soil and seems to disappear. From a distance all that is seen is the body - the neck appears to be buried. Ostriches use the same posture on the nest to protect their young.

Ostriches are born to run; their long bare legs are thick and powerful. The birds can maintain speeds over 30 miles an hour, with strides as long as five yards. If they are unable to outrun danger, adult males can kick hard enough to wound large predators.

Roosters mate with a major hen that lays a clutch of five to 11 eggs in a shallow hollow in the ground. The male may also mate with several minor hens, with each depositing additional eggs in the clutch—the total number can grow to 70 or 80. However, no more than a couple of dozen or so can be covered and incubated. Since only the rooster and the major hen tend the nest and since the latter is able to distinguish which eggs are hers, a small number of eggs laid by the minor hens ever hatch. The dun colored hen sits on the nest during the day and the black rooster covers it at night.

Adult ostriches have advanced immune systems. They also have good vision and, like baboons are often seen intermingled with antelope. The birds' good eyesight and the mammal's keen sense of smell are the basis for a mutually beneficial relationship between the two species.

In my journal I write, "Perhaps the most amazing thing was running into thousands of wildebeest and zebra making the migration to the Maasai Mara in Kenya. I really don't know how to describe it. There were so many animals." Impressed as I was with the size of the herds we view that day, the numbers are actually small compared to those we are to see later in the trip.

The "endless plains" of the Serengeti have the largest concentration of migratory game animals in the world. The combination of the Serengeti, Ngorongoro Conservation Area, four Game Reserves, one Game Controlled area and the Maasai Mara in Kenya provide protection to the largest single movement of wildlife left on earth. Each year, about 1.5 million wildebeest and 500,000 Zebra migrate from the Serengeti in Tanzania to Kenya's Maasai Mara and back, as they follow the rain to green grazing. The herds make a clockwise circle of 1500 miles, the amount of time they spend in any place determined by the available food.

With the short rains in November, the wildebeest move south to the plains of Tanzania - where the grasses are rich in minerals - and drop their calves there. During the peak calving period in February, approximately 8000 wildebeest calves are born every day for ten days in the Western Serengeti. Young born later will be at special risk when the herds begin to migrate. Even those born early in the calving season will find the journey a perilous one, as will all but the fittest of the adults. Lions, hyena and other predators watch the herds closely and are quick to take advantage of the young and the old, the weak and the lost. In addition, many animals fail to successfully navigate the river crossings that lie in the migration's path.

When the rains stop, the plains quickly dry up and in May the wildebeest begin to move north to Kenya and better grazing. Sometimes the migration takes the form of long lines that seem to stretch forever; in other places there are countless animals moving together in huge herds.

The *Wild Lives Guidebook* describes the wildebeest as looking like it was "assembled from spare parts—the forequarters could have come from an ox, the hindquarters from an antelope and the mane and tail from a horse." The large muscular front half of the wildebeest slopes dramatically to a skinny rear end. The body color is gray to brown with darker vertical stripes of hair down the shoulders. A scraggly beard sprouts from the wildebeest's dark wide flat face—which seems to wear a perpetually dumbfounded expression. During the rutting season, territorial males move about in a crazed frenetic way that has led to their being called, "the clowns of the savanna." Watching the animals during the migration is an endlessly entertaining experience—and a noisy one. Wildebeest grunt constantly.

Prior to going on safari, I had envisioned the migration as a kind of stampede; in fact, the wildebeest mostly move in a steady orderly way. If there is food and water where they are, they dawdle. If there is not, they move relentlessly, day and night, at a walk or slow gallop to reach fresh grazing. Occasionally they will run and, when they do, a single wildebeest from a distance looks like something out of a prehistoric cave painting.

On my third safari, our Serengeti tent camp was surrounded by the migration on three sides. It started with a trickle and slowly built until by the time we turned in for the night, there were tens of thousands of animals passing us. The level of noise was incredible; none of us could sleep—but who cared? We had come to see the migration and it was thrilling to find ourselves in the middle of it.

After we retired for the night, some of the animals crept up into camp. I could hear wildebeest grunts and zebra barks right outside my tent. The next day one brave soul who went out to the chemical toilet in the middle of the night told us she had seen many pairs of animal eyes reflected by her flashlight when she swept it over the area. Just before dawn I tentatively unzipped my tent flap a few inches and peered out to see several wildebeest standing about 25 feet away.

We were all out of our tents at first light to watch the seemingly endless mass of animals continue to stream past. As we began to move about, the ones that had been in our camp moved farther away but some of the more brave remained relatively close. I had the surreal experience of brushing my teeth at sunrise on the Serengeti while an audience of three zebra solemnly observed me from a distance of no more than 30 yards.

On this first safari we return to camp for lunch after a full morning in the bush. While we are eating, the staff fills the canvas buckets in the sun showers with warm water. We are delighted to be able to wash off two days of game drive sweat, dust and grit. At the same time, we are aware that for Tanzanians, just getting enough water to drink can be a struggle. With this in mind, we stretch the water so each bucket provides more showers than intended. The staff will drain any unused water and re-heat it on another day.

In the afternoon, a representative from the Serengeti Lion Research Project, which began in 1965, comes to make a presentation about her work. (Back home, I go on the Internet to learn more about the project. It's website www.lionresearch.com shows a photograph of a 35,000 year old drawing of lions found in a cave in France. Under the photo is an excerpt from Samuel Johnson's 1755 *Dictionary of the English Language*, "Lion: The fiercest and most magnanimous of the four footed beasts.")

The researcher talks about collecting data to determine whether female lions have a preference for males with short manes versus long, light manes versus dark. She describes how the females react to the life sized stuffed male lions used in the research. After putting the decoys out in an area where she knows there are female lions nearby, the researcher jumps back in the truck and plays a tape of a roaring lion through a speaker. Slowly the females approach. They try to engage the fake lions, to get them to react to them in some way. Gradually, they become disgusted and start beating the stuffing—literally—out of the imposters. Laughing, our speaker says her decoys are looking pretty sad these days.

The results of the project point to female lions preferring males with long, dark manes. Related research has shown that the longer and darker a lion's mane, the higher the temperatures within it. In order to support the intense heat created by a long, dark mane, a male lion must be very healthy. The supposition of the researchers is that the preference of the female for the long, dark mane has its root in biology and natural selection. Not only are such males more likely to sire healthy cubs but they also are better able to defend their territory. When new males take over a pride, the first thing they usually do is kill the cubs. This causes the females to come into estrus, allowing the new males to create their own reproductive legacy. Healthy males are more likely to be able to fight off challengers and this increases the chance that females in the pride will be able to raise their cubs to maturity.

The researcher is a young blonde woman—slim and attractive. As she is speaking to us, an enormous flying insect hits her chest and falls down into the deep vee-neck of her top. Without missing a beat, she reaches up and grabs the bug through the fabric, crushes it, then pulls the shirt away from her body and shakes it so that the body parts fall to the ground at her feet. Clearly, she is used to life in the bush.

She shows us some of the records the project keeps on the 300 lions that have been catalogued. Every lion has a unique whisker pattern that is documented and used for identification. The researchers have placed a radio collar on one member of twenty-four different Serengeti prides and they try to make contact with each pride once a week. When they immobilize a lion to put on the radio collar, the animal's girth is measured and used to extrapolate body weight. Blood and parasite samples also are taken. Our speaker passes one of the collars around and we are surprised at how heavy it is. Apparently, the lions quickly become used to the weight. On one of my later safaris, I see a lion wearing a collar; she seems as oblivious to it as my dogs are to theirs.

When the afternoon game drive leaves, a few of us stay behind. We nap, read, write in our journals or just sit outside our tents and admire the view. The pace has been very fast and the experiences intense; it is good to take a time out to get centered and reflect on all that has happened so far. Later that night, I write in my journal, "I am glad we are only four days into the adventure, but if it stopped now, it would have been worth the money, the preparation—everything."

By bedtime, it is cold again. The variation in temperature has been significant. We need our jackets at the beginning of the day but in mid-morning we start to shed layers. By noon we are sweaty and glad for our hats as the equatorial sun beats down on us. Around the fire before dinner, we don our jackets again and, when we turn in, we pull the wool blankets on our cots up around us.

Tonight I again hear roaring in the middle of the night, but the noise does not completely rouse me from my slumber. I am becoming accustomed to the sound of lions as I sleep.

# Tano (5)

Today we have an incredible leopard sighting. The vehicle I am in is the first to spot a leopard napping in a tree close to the road. The animal wakes and stands up the minute we stop. It poses briefly in the crook of the tree where it had been sleeping—long enough for me to take several shots. When I have the film developed, I find I have gotten a couple of stunning photographs.

By the time other vehicles begin to arrive, the leopard is on its way down the tree. It passes so close to our vehicle I could have reached out the window and touched it, which I wisely do not attempt to do. Leopards are aloof and secretive animals. If you run across one in a place close enough to get good photographs, it is unlikely to stick around very long.

The leopard population seems to be thriving in Africa. I have read their numbers are greater than those of lion and cheetah combined. This is due in large part to their adaptability in terms of habitat, including being able to thrive in a wide range of temperatures. Leopards are the best climbers of the big cats and their strength enables them to take down prey weighing more than their own 150 pounds. To keep lions and hyenas from stealing their kills, leopards often drag the carcasses up into a tree.

Leopards scratch the trunks of trees with their claws as a message to other leopards to stay away. They are solitary in habit and will fight leopards of the same gender (a male's territory often includes that of several females) that encroach on their territory, which they mark with urine. Leopards share some traits with the common housecats—they spit in fury when they are crossed and they purr when they are relaxed and happy.

The plush soft coats of leopards vary in color depending on where they live—lighter and more golden in warm plains areas and darker for forest dwellers. The fur has irregular spots known as "rosettes". This dappled pattern is very effective camouflage; they are quite difficult for even the most skilled safari guide to locate. Because of that, few things create more excitement on safari than a good leopard sighting.

Not too far from the leopard, we see two healthy looking young lions lounging right by the road. The male is just beginning to get a mane. If he has not already been pushed out of his birth pride, he will be soon. When lions reach two years of age, they are large enough to be independent and the young males are forced to leave the pride by fathers who don't want the competition and by mothers whose instincts are against inbreeding.

Brothers often stay together and eventually use their combined strength to take over a pride. Single males sometimes form coalitions of two or three for the same purpose. It is unusual for more than three males to share a pride; however, there is one on the Serengeti that is controlled by a coalition of seven brothers. For two or three years after they are evicted from their birth prides, groups of several males band together in a nomadic existence. They wander on the edge of other lions' territories, often having to resort to hunting small game like rabbit to survive. By the time they reach four or five years of age, they generally are ready to attempt to take over a pride.

The fight for prides is brutal and can result in the death of one or more of the combatants. As mentioned earlier, when new males take over a pride, they usually kill the cubs. A mother sometimes fights to the death to try to protect her babies. A female lion's investment in her offspring is significant. The gestation period is three months and the cubs, which are born completely helpless, are kept hidden for three months after birth. It is not unusual for a female to go through pregnancy after pregnancy without being able to raise any of her cubs to maturity. The mortality rate for lion cubs is estimated to be as high as 85%.

The average lifespan for a female lion is 14 years; for a male, it is 12. In 2000, the oldest Serengeti lion was a 17-year-old female. There is a project underway to vaccinate dogs around the perimeter of the park against canine distemper and rabies because these diseases currently pose the biggest threats to Serengeti lions. After reaching their lowest numbers in the 1960's, lion numbers in the park are now at an all time high

After the sighting of the two young lions, we make a "pit stop" at the Seronera Serengeti Lodge to take advantage of the restroom facilities and to check out the gift shop. Ruth tells us it would have cost less for us to stay in this nice hotel than in our classic tented camp because the latter is so labor intensive. There is no existing infrastructure; everything has to be transported out to the bush, set up, maintained and taken down again when the group leaves. The opportunity to sleep under canvas was one of the things that drew me to the safari and I think the same is true for almost everyone in our group.

The only holdout might be Betty who is on the trip with her retired husband Ed. Betty is one of those beautifully groomed women who never have a hair out of place. Doing without running water and electricity is not her idea of a good time. However, even in the absence of these grooming basics, she is managing to look much cleaner and neater than the rest of us. Whether that is due to her effort or our lack of it, I can't say.

The camp manager, Antoine, and his workers surprise us with a fabulous hot lunch under a lovely acacia tree. One of the staff pours water over our hands when we arrive. I later learn this is a traditional Tanzanian way of washing up before a meal, a ritual that makes sense in a country where so many homes lack running water.

In the afternoon we visit the Seronera Museum where the story of the migration is told in marvelous exhibits and displays. The museum is built up against a large kopje that features an enormous Candelabra tree. There are a number of impressive metal sculptures on the grounds, including a life size Nile crocodile I especially like. A picnic area with concrete tables is swarming with more varieties of birds than I can count. Those I recognize include red and yellow speckled barbets, brightly colored bee-eaters, superb starlings, and an assortment of thrushes and weavers. The small gift shop offers some items handcrafted by local women who receive a share of the sale proceeds; I buy several sweetly fragrant coiled baskets made of grass. Some of our group purchase lukewarm Cokes and pay $4.00 for tins of Pringles chips at an adjoining snack bar.

We stay in the bush all day, from just after dawn until 7:00 p.m. It is almost dark when we get back to camp. The drivers have radioed ahead so there is warm water waiting for us in our canvas sinks. However, since the staff is busy fixing dinner, they can't heat water for showers. A few brave souls bite the bullet and use the cold water left in the bags from yesterday. A strong breeze is causing the already cool temperatures to drop; most of us decide being grimy is better than freezing. After giving our faces and hands a once over, we reconvene in the dining tent to visit about the day and to enjoy yet another great meal.

My duffle was waiting for me when I got back to camp so I finally have pajamas. When I turn in, I wonder if the popping of the tent in the wind will keep me awake. It doesn't—when someone says the next morning that the lions had been active again during the night, I have to take their word for it.

# Sita (6)

Today is "lion on a rock day". We see them on several kopjes. After gorging themselves from a successful early morning hunt, lions sometimes sprawl on the sun warmed rocks and sleep off their feast. When they wake, being perched on top of a kopje allows them to look out over the plains to observe the herds and scope out their next meal.

On my 2004 safari, we pass a kopje where two lions trying to nap are being harassed by a troop of baboons. Apparently, the baboons consider the kopje their personal territory and they do not intend to share it with lions. They are making a terrible racket, shrieking and running at the cats, while staying just out of reach. Even the little babies are getting into it. Occasionally a baboon throws a rock or a stick at the lions. One of the cats gives a lazy roar—more irritated than aggressive. She stands up, making us think she might be going to attack the baboons. Instead, she turns around and disappears down the other side of the kopje. Baboons one, lions zero.

The baboons, energized by their partial victory, turn all of their combined attention on the remaining lion. When she tries to ignore them, putting her head down and closing her eyes, the baboons ratchet up the noise level and jump around frantically, peppering the big cat with whatever they can find to throw. The lion gives a couple of half-hearted roars but, finally, she gets up and follows her sister down the opposite side of the kopje. Game, set, and match to the baboons.

Later that same day, we pass the kopje again. At first we don't see any animals. Then a couple of lions come into view. One of them has something in her mouth that appears to be baboon hair; it looks like the baboons may not have won after all. However, after a careful check through his binoculars, the driver tells us the hair is too black to be baboon—that it is a piece of wildebeest tail. Whatever it is, it seems to be stuck on the lion's teeth; she shakes her head like she is trying to get rid of it but it remains in place. When we drive away, she is lying on top of the kopje, the wildebeest tail hanging over her chin making her look like a bearded lady.

On this first safari we sight a large group of lions napping on a kopje, not far from where other members of the pride are still feeding at a kill. Vultures are hovering nearby waiting for leftovers. Lions are not the only predators whose hunts have been successful. We observe a Vereaux eagle owl in a tree as it tears into a guinea fowl it has killed. The owl's serenely beautiful visage belies the viciousness with which it is using its beak to rip into the flesh of its prey. We are both disgusted and fascinated.

There are flocks of guinea fowl everywhere in Tanzania. They are beautiful birds but the size of their extremely tiny heads apparently doesn't allow for much brainpower. I have seen them run for a very long way in front of us trying to get away from our vehicles—rather than simply moving to the side of the road.

We also see a baboon with an impala kill. I did not realize that baboons were carnivores but on safari I learn they are opportunistic predators. A large baboon can successfully hunt a small impala. Baboons and impala have a symbiotic relationship; you often see groups of them together because they have complementary strengths. The impalas have good senses of smell and hearing; the baboons have visual acuity and their ability to climb trees gives them a better view of approaching threats. The two species warn each other of danger but, at the same time, enjoy an uneasy truce.

Impalas are so plentiful that they don't get a lot of attention—at least from safari goers; they are highly favored by predators (except for lion who prefer larger prey if it is available). However, few sights on safari are more splendid than that of a group of running impala. The animal is sometimes referred to as the "Maasai Antelope" because it can spring high into the air from a stationery position. Watching a group of impala move when they have been startled (and they are easily startled—understandably perhaps since they have so many enemies) is a grand experience. Their leaps are so explosive it is as though they have been shot from cannons. In mid-air, their legs extend straight from their bodies so that they are stretched into an almost flat line.

Impala have an unusual gland on their fetlocks that distributes a scent along the ground. This allows the animals to find their way back to one another after fleeing in response to a threat. Without it, I am sure many impala babies would end up lost and abandoned. When a group of impala is alarmed, they take off in every direction like popcorn kernels being heated in a pan without a lid. This forces a predator to make a choice about which animal to follow. If the object of his attack escapes, he can't simply turn his attention to another one nearby. However, it also makes it essential that impala have a way to find their way back together again.

At the site of the impala kill, several marabou storks are watching the baboon eating, waiting for their chance at what is left when he finishes. Storks are ancient birds; the fossil evidence dates them back 50 million years. However, although she has had eons to get it right, the marabou stork is not Mother Nature's best work in the beauty department. While the word "marabou" conjures images of a glamorous feather boa, the bird from which the feathers come is about as far from "glamorous" as you can get. The marabou stork is one ugly critter!

Marabous resemble vultures more than they do the idealized stork image of a snowy white bird with long graceful legs. Actually, the marabou's hollow black legs are long—but they don't score many points on the beauty scale because they are usually so thickly coated in excrement as to appear white. Their almost bald heads and naked necks are a mottled pinkish-red, their conically shaped bills are comically oversized and their heavy bodies are covered with dark gray feathers on the top and white underneath. (The soft white tail feathers are the ones used in boas.) I call them "Boris Karloff" birds because they look like something out of a horror movie—and also because when they are taking off and landing, their wings make a creaking noise very similar to movie sound effects for the opening of a door in a haunted house.

Even if you are a subscriber to the "pretty is as pretty does theory", the marabou falls short; its behaviors can be as unappealing as its physical appearance. For example, the bird is attracted to grassfires because it can stage itself just ahead of the flames and pick off small animals as they flee. It also has been known to stampede flamingos so it can grab any chicks that fall behind. However marabous primarily feed on carrion, garbage and other rotting material.

The marabou stork is at heart a scavenger and its eating habits give it a valuable role in sub-Saharan East Africa. Many villages and towns encourage the presence of the birds because by consuming garbage and rubbish, they help to keep the environment clean, to control rodents and to prevent the spread of pathogens. Essentially, they are sanitation workers. In the bush the marabou's powerful beak allows it to pierce the thick hides of large carcasses, speeding decomposition and giving smaller animals access to food. This is an important contribution in an ecosystem where a carcass can be that of an elephant weighing several tons.

There are other things about marabous that fall into the "don't judge a book by the cover" category. They are outgoing, gregarious and social birds, sometimes becoming quite tame in situations where they have frequent contact with people. There are stories of marabous making regular trips to the local dump and hanging out near slaughterhouses waiting for the workers to toss them scraps. They sometimes build their stick nests in towns.

Marabous are four to five feet tall, the largest of the storks. They have a wingspread of ten feet - only slightly less than a condor's—and they are impressive flyers. At about four years of age they mate for life. Both males and females are conscientious parents; they take turns keeping the eggs warm and feeding the down-covered white chicks, which are helpless when they hatch. Like all storks, marabous communicate by clacking or rattling their beaks. However, the marabou stork has an inflatable throat pouch that also allows it to produce a guttural croak.

Probably the most common stork in East Africa today, marabous were becoming scarce in the early 20th century. The growth in their numbers is related to the waste that has accompanied increases in the human population—and to a drop in popularity of marabou feathers as a fashion accent.

The highlight of today's safari is seeing more of the migration. From a distance the lines of wildebeest look like unending streams of ants. At a watering hole, we see not only a large number of wildebeest, but also hartebeest, one of the fastest antelopes and the one with the most endurance, waterbuck with its longish, almost shaggy coat, and glossy topi standing in the shade chewing their cud. Fearing unseen crocodiles lurking beneath the surface, the animals are skittish around the water.

In another location, the front of a long line of wildebeest suddenly stops its steady movement forward, forming a bunched up cluster that grows larger as more and more of the line reaches the most forward point. Using our binoculars to try to determine what has caused the animals to halt so suddenly, we see two lions in front of the wildebeest. The latter retreat and, interestingly, so do the lions. Clearly, it was just an accidental encounter rather than an ambush.

One of our drivers finds a fresh carcass in a tree. It is the body of a wildebeest—a small one, but still it is hard to imagine how a leopard had managed to drag him up there. When it is pointed out to me, I can see the dead animal but I never would have spotted it on my own. It is another example of how good the drivers are at what they do. Following the tree line, we soon come upon the leopard that killed the wildebeest. Less than thrilled to see us, the animal quickly disappears into the underbrush.

We locate an acacia with a large shady canopy for today's picnic lunch. When we arrive, we disrupt a tall giraffe munching on the leaves. Giraffes have leathery tongues that make it possible for them to eat around the needle sharp thorns on acacias. Before going on safari, I had only seen giraffes in zoos where the confined space made them seem clumsy and awkward, like overgrown adolescents. On the wide plains of the Serengeti, I was astonished to discover that giraffes run with a rhythmic, hypnotic grace. I never tire of watching them.

Early cave paintings of *"Twiga"* or giraffe are evidence of the long fascination the animal has had for mankind. When Africa was first opened to the outside world, giraffe were regarded as such curiosities that they were sometimes given as prized gifts from one nation or ruler to another. The African Wildlife Foundation's *Wild Lives Guidebook,* refers to "Early written records" that describe the giraffe as "magnificent in appearance, bizarre in form, unique in gait, colossal in height and inoffensive in character."

I will always remember an evening on my second safari when we came upon 32 giraffe gliding across the plains with the setting sun as a backdrop. Because the light was fading and we were on our way back to camp, I had already put my camera away. I didn't even think about pulling it back out again. The scene was one of those absolutely perfect moments and I didn't want anything to come between me and the experience.

Today, we go back early so we can take showers and organize our stuff for tomorrow's departure. Now that my duffle has caught up with me, I have more clothes than I need so I put some aside to leave behind for the staff. Ruth had advised us to bring old clothes we could give away at the end of the safari; I am just starting to discard things early.

Today is Ruth's birthday. We improvise a party for her at dinner, giving her gifts from our luggage like paperbacks and gum. The menu of traditional African foods contributes to the festive atmosphere. I have never eaten bananas in a stew before—the dish is surprisingly good. The finishing touch is a birthday cake, made like everything else on an open fire. The staff entertains us with songs and skits after dinner and then surprises us with champagne.

Champagne in a candlelit tent on the Serengeti—definitely something to remember! We linger a bit after dinner aware this is our last night on the endless plains. We are feeling both sad to be leaving and eager to move on to the adventures that lie ahead.

It is a beautiful night; the moon is full and so bright we don't need flashlights for our pre-bed visits to the toilets. (On a night much like this on a later trip, it is so clear we can see the rings of Saturn through one of our trip mate's very powerful high tech binoculars.)

Tomorrow we bid goodbye— *"kwa heri"* in Swahili - to the Serengeti, place of legend and adventure, of dreams and promise, of life and death, of yesterday, today and forever.

# Saba (7)

We weren't scheduled to leave camp until 7:30 so, by safari standards at least, we got to sleep in this morning. Because we have a long drive ahead of us today, the vehicle tops are closed. On our way out of the park, we see a group of eight lions, one of them lying in the middle of the road. We also pass three cheetahs running single file across the savannah. Even if the top had been open, we would not have been able to get photos—they are gone in a flash.

Cheetahs have been clocked at 70 miles per hour, much faster than lions and leopards. However, they are sprinters and can't run for great distances without becoming overheated. Shrinking habitat and high cub mortality are steadily reducing cheetah numbers and the cat already has disappeared from southern Asia, the Middle East, India and much of Africa.

The cheetahs we see disappear beyond a stand of acacia. These trees are the most prominent foliage on the Serengeti plains. There are hundreds of varieties of acacia, the majority of which are located in Australia and Africa. Often called "thorn" or "umbrella" trees, acacias play a number of roles in sub-Saharan Africa.

The trees are incredibly well adapted to their environment; the ability to adjust the position of their leaves depending on whether they need to absorb sunlight or conserve moisture is vital in allowing them to survive hot dry conditions. The trees have many small leaves; leaves with a large surface area would require more shade and moisture than are available in their habitat.

Acacias are a food source for many browsers—from tall giraffes to tiny ants. The relationship between cocktail ants and the whistling acacia is an interesting one. About 20% of this tree's thorns are swollen at the base to create a gall. The ants pierce the gall and live inside. The tree gets its name from the whistling sound the wind makes when it blows through the holes in the galls.

The ants feed on the sap from the acacia leaves. In exchange for their room and board, they police the branches of the tree chasing away beetles, grasshoppers, and caterpillars by biting them. Even giraffe and rhino can be so discomfited by the ants that they sometimes move on to another tree. This helps to prevent over-browsing. The ants are least active during the time of day when bees are at their busiest; this allows for essential cross-pollination. Mother Nature thinks of everything.

Acacias have of necessity developed other defenses. Some of them have both straight and hooked thorns, which serve as deterrents to different animals and the acacia's many small leaflets assure that the trees will not be completely stripped. Some varieties of acacia release tannins, which make their leaves unappetizing.

The Wildwatch website states "that soil fertility is higher below the canopies of acacia trees, due to leaf-fall and decomposition, and the accumulation of droppings from roosting birds and from herbivores seeking shade." In other words, acacias have a role in improving the soil.

Many Tanzanians use acacia for fuel, burning the wood or charcoal made from it. As populations increase, it is important to manage such use in order to protect the long-term viability of the trees. The beauty, adaptability, quirkiness, cunning, multiple talents and resilience of the acacia make it a perfect symbol for East Africa.

Before a scheduled visit to a Maasai boma, or village, we stop so Ruth can give us a short talk on the Maasai and their culture. We learn their diet consists primarily of milk, to which blood is added on special occasions. Livestock, especially cattle, are at the center of Maasai life. In some areas, Maasai are beginning to farm; however the traditional view is that tilling the soil is a crime against nature because it makes the land unsuitable for grazing. Scant water in the bush makes cleanliness a challenge for the Maasai; they clean their gourd pots with urine, which is sterile when it leaves the body.

Ruth explains she will be making a donation to the boma on our behalf in exchange for the Massai allowing us to take their photos and to tour one of their huts. We also have brought school supplies for the children. As Ruth is speaking, we hear cowbells drawing near. A few minutes later, a Maasai passes us with a herd of cattle and goats. It is a perfectly timed visual.

The boma we are visiting is in an arid, isolated location at the base of a majestic, moody looking mountain. It is an overcast day and in the gray light the sky is a deep teal blue with many puffy two-tone clouds— stormy dark on the top and cotton ball white underneath. The village consists of a circle of huts made of dung, sticks and mud. Surrounding the huts is a thick fence of thorn trees with a narrow opening. Livestock are sometimes herded into the center of the boma for safekeeping at night.

The chief comes out to greet us and escorts us into the village. There, the young men dance for us in the traditional Maasai fashion. Standing ramrod straight, holding a spear in one hand, both arms pressed firmly to their sides, they leap up to improbable heights. They seem to defy the laws of gravity as they jump higher and higher, competing to out-do one another. As they dance, they chant, creating a deep resonant sound.

The dancers are Morani—warriors—the best-looking, most favored bachelors in the tribe. As they jump, their intricately braided hairstyles and heavy beaded earrings bounce, their bracelets glitter in the sun. Behind veiled eyes, the unmarried Maasai girls watch in admiration. Our presence is just an excuse; the Morani are really dancing for these lovely young women.

When the men's performance ends, a group of women starts to dance. Unlike the male dancers, these females are married rather than single. Some dance with infants on their backs, toddlers on their hips, children at their knees. They don't leap as high as the men and, instead of keeping their bodies rigidly straight, they thrust forward so the bright beaded collars layered around their long slender neck bounce wildly. In contrast to the elaborate hairstyles of the Morani, their heads are shaved smooth.

Some of them grab the hands of women in our group and try to pull us into the dance. We say "no" and shake our heads but they are insistent. Laughing, we give our cameras and hats to our trip mates. In the photos, even the skinniest women in our group look heavy beside the blade slender Maasai women—and the video evidence shows us to be painfully clumsy compared to their lithe, effortless grace.

When the dancing is over, we are taken in small groups into one of the mud and dung huts where the Maasai live. We must bend low to enter the doorway. The interior is dead dark; the entire time I am inside, my eyes never adjust to the blackness. The fire in the center of the room is not lit but smoke from past fires is sharp in the air, causing my eyes to water and blur. In the small, closed space the acrid odor of old smoke is mixed with smells of people who never wash, of animals, of curdled milk and blood—my stomach becomes queasy and I leave before the "tour" is over. It is a relief to get back to the light and the open air.

The women of the village have set up a shopping area where they offer their handcrafts for sale. There are beaded bracelets, pendants, earrings, collars, belts and hunting clubs with beaded trim. Each woman, sometimes with the assistance of a husband or son, is in charge

own small area. They are very aggressive. When we admire
ning, they immediately try to put it on us or into our hands. If
they are successful, they refuse to take the merchandise back. I enlist
Nickson's help to negotiate for the beaded collar and club I want to buy.
Once I have paid for my purchases, I leave the shopping area and wait
for the rest of the group by the opening in the thorn fence.

There are small, unsupervised children everywhere. Perhaps because
they are closer to the ground, they seem to be covered in even thicker
layers of dust than are the adults. Many of them have on dirty, ragged
Western clothes. I suspect if we were not there, they might be naked.
One toddler wears a shift like garment; as he runs across the center of
the boma, he pulls it to one side and pees on the go. Flies are thick on
the children's faces, especially around their eyes. In her talk about the
Maasai, Ruth told us the children often have eye problems because of
the flies, the smoke in the huts and the ever-present dust. The Maasai
love their children but they do not coddle them. Life in the bush is hard
and there is no place for a child who cannot withstand its rigors.

I cannot imagine living this way but it is my sense the Maasai feel
the same—that they are no more interested than we are in trading
their lives for ours. We feel superior because of all the things we have
that they lack, because their lives are so hard—but they do not seem
unhappy. No running water, electricity, flush toilets, shopping malls,
SUV's, movies, TV, cable, restaurants, Botox, treadmills, tanning
booths, microwaves, convenience stores, icemakers, garbage disposals,
Wonderbras, Viagra, fax machines or cell phones. The list of what they
don't have is unending. We have spent our lives acquiring things as the
path to happiness. It is unnerving to think they might be happier with
virtually nothing than we are with virtually everything.

When we leave the boma, we head north to the highland area of
Karatu. Our first stop is for a late lunch at Gibb's Farm, a guest lodge
and restaurant on a working coffee plantation. The food is spectacular;
many of the ingredients are from the lodge gardens. The building in
which the dining room is located is uncluttered and open, with glowing
wood floors, creamy white stucco walls and spare, carefully chosen
decor. After eating, we go outside to have coffee on a rolling green
lawn surrounded by flowers and overlooking a view of the hills below,
many of them planted with coffee. Like the other plantations and lodges
in the area, Gibb's Farm is owned by whites. It is easy to see why colonists
would have settled here. It is the Garden of Eden with a perfect climate,
rich soil and cheap labor. We leave reluctantly, wishing we were staying
at this storybook place.

When we get to Kifaru (The word means "rhino" in Swahili.)
Lodge, our home for the next two nights, we realize we should have

had more confidence in Ruth. Like Gibb's Farm, Kifaru is beautifully landscaped and boasts gorgeous views. The sleeping rooms are located in several different freestanding buildings, each with its own name and personality. I am in the "Tea House" which has three or four bedrooms around a shared living area that is furnished in a vaguely Japanese style. There are vases and bowls of fresh flowers everywhere, all of them picked from the lodge gardens. I have a charming room with a single bed and an adjoining tiled bath. The lodge uses a wood fire to power its water heater so hot water is available 24 hours a day. A generator provides electricity for about two hours in the morning and again in the evening.

The drive had been long, hot and dusty so we waste no time taking advantage of the hot water. After showering, most of us go on a guided walk around the grounds. Near a garden, we pass a long wire with pieces of metal tied to it. Our guide explains that a guard is posted at night and, when he sees an elephant approaching the field, he tugs on the wire causing the pieces of metal to clang against one another and make a racket. This frightens the elephant away from the vegetables. A few minutes after this explanation, we see a lone elephant in the distance headed our way. He should be here by nightfall.

As we walk past fields of coffee plants covered with green fruit, children come out of huts where they live with their parents who work on the plantation. They run up to us waving and smiling. One boy asks us for a pencil. The thick grass is tall in places and the guide uses a machete to clear a path to our destination, which is a small picturesque waterfall. The walk back is a steady uphill slope that leaves us short of breath.

By the time we arrive at the lodge, we are hot and sweaty again but it was worth it. One of the downsides of going on safari is the limited opportunity for physical activity. You are in the vehicles for long hours, either on the road or in the parks. This opportunity to stretch our legs has been very welcome.

We convene in the lodge main house, a light and airy building with a number of wonderful batiks by Swedish artist Heidi Lange on the walls. Lange specializes in studies of East African life in detailed black and white on tie dyed cotton. Her work is very distinctive and is widely available in Tanzania and Kenya.

Afreida, who manages Kifaru for its German owners, calls us to dinner. The meal is worthy of any five star restaurant in the world. In fact, every meal at Kifaru is delicious and beautifully presented. On my 2001 trip, I stay behind one day to enjoy the lodge and its grounds while the rest of the group goes on an outing. I tell Alfreida I will just have the same box lunch she sends with the group but she won't hear of it. The kitchen makes spaghetti with a perfectly seasoned homemade sauce—and, for dessert, a warm crepe spread with jam. Alfreida takes me on a tour of the kitchen and I see it has no modern conveniences—everything is done by hand. My cooking is not even half as good—and I have almost every appliance known to the to civilized world.

On my first night at Kifaru, the generator is off when I return to my room after dinner, so I brush my teeth by flashlight. After four nights on a camp cot, the mattress feels very luxurious. As I snuggle into the pillow, it occurs to me that there is no lock on my bedroom door. In a hotel back in the states that would be cause for concern, but here it is nothing to lose sleep over.

# Nane (8)

We have a long drive today so we get up very early. After a generous breakfast of bacon, eggs, toast, juice and coffee made from fresh roasted beans grown on the lodge grounds, we head off for a visit with the Hadza bush people. Alternatively spelled Hadzapi and Hadzabe and also known as the Tindinga or Kindinga, this tribe dates back to the Stone Age. The 400 or so members of the Eastern Hadza living in Tanzania today are the only hunter-gatherers left in Africa. Hunting and gathering was the way all mankind lived for the bulk of human history; it is less than 15,000 years since we began to domesticate plants and animals. The Hadza are throwbacks to another era; they live much as our ancestors did at the dawn of human time.

Our destination today is Lake Eyasi in northern Tanzania. The Hadza live in this hot dry area in small groups of adults and children that move every couple of weeks. In wet weather, they set up camp in caves, some of which have been used by the Hadza for thousands of years. More often, their shelter consists of transient round structures constructed by the Hadza women of bent branches woven together and covered with grass. It only takes the women a couple of hours to build a new camp.

The Hadza have resisted government efforts to mainstream them. They live in the moment and have shown no inclination to settle down in permanent homes and raise crops. A major relocation effort in the 1960's provided the Hadza with housing, food, clean water and medical care. The Hadza did not flourish and by the 1980's almost all of them had returned to life in the bush. Their children do not attend school and the Hadza do not pay taxes. As "progress" places increasing pressure on their lifestyles and habitat, there are concerns that if the Hadza are not mainstreamed, they are doomed to disappear. Some of the men do move back and forth between Hadza life and mainstream culture but the net effect seems to be negative in that it brings some of the threats of modern life—e.g. diseases—to the Hadza without doing much to integrate them into contemporary society.

To get to the area where the Hadza live, we drive for hours through billowing red dust so thick our vision is often obscured. The heat is stifling but we have to keep the windows closed much of the time because of the dust. The road is an obstacle course of rocks, bumps and gaping crevasses. Several times we jolt so hard that my head hits the ceiling of the vehicle. Finally, we come to a small village that looks poorer than anything we have seen so far. Every structure is ramshackle and, of course, covered with layers of dust. Three of our vehicles are to wait here while the fourth goes to pick up our guide-interpreter for the Hadza.

We soon attract the attention of a small horde of village children. They sit in a line on a low wall close to our vehicles and watch us. Kris, a recent college graduate, entertains them with his hackey sack skills. They are drawn to his youth and energy and tall good looks. Then Sandy, who to this point has seemed a practical, no nonsense type, sits down in the middle of the children and begins to sing "Frere Jacques", causing them to giggle. One beautiful little girl with a brilliant smile on her very dirty face has a baby tied to her back in a faded kanga. No more than seven or eight years old, she seems unaware of her burden, a sign she is accustomed to it.

Two young women watch us from the doorway of a nearby hut. The brightness of their boldly patterned kanga skirts and head wraps is jarring in this dingy, dust covered, dun colored setting. The aged decrepit building we are parked by has a sign that says "Hotel". I take a photo and when I return home, tell family and friends this is where I stayed. They believe me.

Finally, the fourth vehicle returns with Mamoya, our guide. He is a member of the Watoga tribe but he speaks the click language of the Hadza. Just as importantly, he knows where in the hundreds of square miles around Lake Eyasi we are likely to find the Hadza group we are seeking. Mamoya directs the drivers to an area where they park the vehicles and we all get out and walk the rest of the way. It is hot and dry and the land seems utterly inhospitable. After the equivalent of several city blocks, we come upon five or six men and four women. We see no shelters or evidence of camp and there are no children present. These adults have apparently been selected to meet with us away from the others.

After a brief conversation, Mamoya explains the group has just completed a meal of baboon. He points out a young man who has a strip of bloody animal skin tied around his forehead; it identifies him as the hunter who killed the baboon. The men are making arrows; Mamoya tells us the points have not yet been dipped in poison so they are safe for us to handle. Markings scratched onto the arrow shafts identify the man to whom they belong.

Some of the people in our group negotiate to buy arrows to take home as souvenirs. Most pay with shillings but Ed barters his hat for two arrows. It is a good deal for Ed only because he has another hat back at the lodge; sun protection for your head is a critical piece of equipment on safari. (Since this experience, I have read that there is supposed to be no trading when tourists visit the Hadza. At one time, this was a rule that the government was intent upon enforcing but if that was still the case when we visited, we were unaware of it.)

For some reason, the Hadza man Mamoya says is the chief for this group (Actually, the Hadza have no chiefs per se; this man was the eldest present and perhaps that made him the spokesperson by default.) pantomimes for me to try his bow. Years ago, I taught archery in summer playground programs so I welcome the opportunity to demonstrate my prowess. My arrogance is short lived. Even though I am a head taller than the chief, I can pull the animal tendon string of his bow back only a few inches.

All of the Hadza men are of fairly small stature but they are very muscular. When they do a target shooting demonstration for us, they draw their bows with a goose bump inspiring combination of grace and strength. Kris tries his hand at target practice and makes a good showing.

The four women—one is really just a girl; she looks to be no older than 16 year old Lauren in our group—sit in a semi-circle on the ground and speak to us through Mamoya. He translates our questions and interprets the women's replies. At one point, we invite them to ask questions of us. The oldest of the women, says, "If you have no land and you raise no crops or animals and you do not hunt for your meat, what do you eat?" Our explanations of supermarkets make so sense to them.

On the ground near the women is a crude doll made of dried mud. Mamoya explains it is a child's toy. When one of us picks it up, the head falls off. We are appalled but the women laugh and Mamoya assures us there is no harm done; another is easily made. This seems to be the underlying theme of Hadza life. Permanence is not highly valued.

Hadza are welcoming to visitors, especially groups like ours who pay for the opportunity to meet with them. Ruth has been told they use the money to pay for basics the bush does not provide. However, for countless generations, the Hadza have been able to live off the land without commercial purchases. We later learn one of the things this group buys with the money we give them is marijuana.

On my 2001 safari, the Hadza men our group visits are smoking marijuana while we are there. They pass a pipe around their circle, each man taking a deep hit and then convulsing into a spell of violent coughing. On this same visit, one of the bushmen offers six baboons and a log of honey if a woman in our group will become one of his wives. It is a joke but not really; the woman is a beautiful blonde and if she had accepted, I think he would have been glad to part with the baboons and the honey.

After the archery demonstration we hike back to our vehicles, chattering about what we have seen and learned in our time with the Hadza. Those of us who have bought or bartered for arrows begin to think about the logistics of getting them home on the plane. We drive to Lake Eyasi and eat our box lunches in a small scrubby patch of shade. The area around this soda lake is desolate and there is not much to see. After some remarks by Mamoya about his Watoga tribe, we settle into the vehicles for the ride back to Kifaru.

Our driver, Kennedy, decides to take a shortcut and gets stuck in thick ooze that lies just under the dry surface. The other three trucks come back to help free us. We don't have what we need to be towed out of the sticky gray muck so the women gather rocks and the men pile them under the tires. We are in the middle of a large flat area with no underbrush or trees. A strong hot wind coming off the lake picks up little pieces of sandy salt grit, blowing them into our skin; they feel like fire pellets hitting our arms and legs. It is a long, uncomfortable hour but eventually we are on our way again.

For some reason—perhaps because we are hot and tried and grumpy—the drive back seems much longer and more unpleasant. In my journal I write, "Drive back horrendous. Red dust so thick—road a nightmare."

Finally, we get back to the lodge where a late afternoon tea is waiting for us on the lush side lawn adjacent to the main house. We shower and then come back together for yet another perfectly prepared gourmet meal; the spinach pie appetizer is sublime. After dinner, Alfreida distributes the laundry we had left to be done. Because everything is still damp, those of us in the Tea House spread our washed clothes out all over the living area to finish drying overnight. Before turning in, I pack up for tomorrow's departure. I have bought several bags of coffee beans to take back as gifts; they fill my room and my luggage with a deep earthy aroma.

The day's experiences have been worth the difficulties. If I had known this morning how exhausting the drive was going to be, I still would have gone. The chance to get a glimpse of what life was like for our distant ancestors was priceless—and more than worth some inconvenience. We had not been able to manage with good grace for less than a day in the world the Hadza inhabit full time. As with the Maasai, I did not get the sense they would trade their lives for ours if the opportunity were offered. It was something to think about—but not tonight.

# Tisa (9)

I slept soundly through last night's heavy rains so it is a surprise to wake to a very foggy, wet world. I am glad to have the plastic collapsible rain hat I tossed into my luggage at the last minute. Its wide brim offers good protection and it is less cumbersome than an umbrella. I need my hands free in order to wrestle my duffle outside to the porch so the staff can load it for today's journey.

I give Alfreida some extra toiletries, a tee shirt and other things I am sure I won't need. Although she is very young, she is a natural nurturer and Ruth says she helps many people in the community. I know she will find someone who will be grateful for my castoffs. It is sobering to realize our extras and leftovers represent abundance for many Tanzanians.

Last night's rain means there is no dust today but the big news is paved roads. After yesterday, the relatively smooth ride is very welcome. We stop at a small bank to change money and then visit a school. Only the 7th grade class is in session but the school grounds are full of children of all ages who apparently are there to see us. Their parents pay tuition for them to attend the school and, although some of their clothing shows wear, they are relatively clean and well dressed compared to what we have seen in other places. Kris quickly becomes the center of attention when he joins a group of boys kicking around a soccer ball. A circle of admirers surrounds him as he does tricks with the ball.

The students in the 7th grade classroom are studying for the upcoming National Exams. This one test will have a big impact on their future. Those who do not qualify for secondary school will not be able to continue their education.

Education for all of its citizens is Tanzania's most cherished goal. The country claims to have had a literacy rate of over 90% before an attempted invasion by Idi Amin in 1978. Tanzania repelled the invasion, driving Amin back into Uganda and—in cooperation with armed Ugandan exiles—deposing the dictator. Although successful, the effort bankrupted Tanzania, negatively impacting attainment of its goal of universal literacy. Today, the literacy rate in Tanzania is 78% compared to 97% for the United States.

Tanzania's first president, the beloved Julius Nyerere, was a teacher by profession and is affectionately referred to as *"Mwalimu"* (Swahili for "teacher") by the populace. Early in his presidency, Nyerere directed 14% of the country's budget to education. He made primary education not only free, but also compulsory. Today, only two or three percent of children go on to secondary school. Cost is a factor —secondary school tuition is prohibitive for many families—but so is availability of resources for secondary education. Primary schools also are facing challenges. To try to improve the situation, the government is encouraging the establishment of more private schools. All of our driver guides send their children to private schools.

School visits have been part of each of my trips to Tanzania. Most of the classrooms have been modest at best and some have been in serious disrepair. With 50, 60—even 70 children in a class, four and five students were crowded on hard wooden benches intended for two. There were none of the colorful posters and "teaching aids" that are standard fare in U. S. schools. The students did not have fancy notebooks with Velcro closures and photographs of MTV stars on the covers. There were no electric pencil sharpeners; in most classrooms there were no books

The schools I have visited in Tanzania had little more than well-behaved children who were eager to learn and dedicated teachers who were proud to teach. In every classroom, we were greeted with music, the students singing in clear, melodic voices as a way to welcome us. In fact, the song we heard most often was "We Are Happy to Say Welcome."

In the 7th grade classroom we visit on the drive from Kifaru, the teacher invites us each to introduce ourselves to the students. I decide to give my language skills a try and make my introductions in Swahili. I am delighted when the students understand me. However, I have a long way to go before my Swahili is as good as their English.

My Swahili has improved with each visit to Africa. My original thought was that knowing a bit of the language was a way to show respect for the country I was visiting. However, I think my limited knowledge of Swahili has enriched my safari experience. It has sparked some interactions that would not have otherwise occurred.

Once, in a market in Zanzibar, our group passed a very elderly man sitting on an overturned red plastic bucket. The people ahead of me all said *"Jambo"* which is a kind of pigeon Swahili for "hello". When I reached the old man, I greeted him with *"Shikamoo"*, an expression of respect used only when meeting an honored elder or a person of importance. His eyes lit up and his face broke out in an ear-to-ear toothless smile. We exchanged a few polite phrases in Swahili—nothing profound. What we said was not as important as the fact that we were two human beings of vastly different cultures who experienced a moment of connection—all because I knew one little word in another language.

After visiting the 7th graders, we walk back through the crowded schoolyard to our vehicles. Many of the children ask us for gum, pencils, or pens. Our pre-safari instructions had told us that we should not give handouts to children because it encouraged them to beg. Rather it was suggested that we bring school supplies to be pooled and donated to schools we visited on our journey.

When children asked for things like gum, candy or money, I was okay with saying "no." When they asked for pencils, I felt less comfortable refusing. How could it be harmful to give a child something that he needed for his schoolwork? However, according to the drivers, many of the children who ask for pens and pencils end up selling them. They have learned that tourists are more likely to give them those kinds of things than money—but, in the end, it is the same thing.

I am the first person to get back to our Land Rover. A handsome boy with a scrubbed face and enormous eyes asks me to take his photograph. At first, I decline but he is very insistent. Not understanding why it is so important to him for me to take a picture he will never see, I finally give in and comply. As soon as I snap the photo, the boy thrusts out his hand and asks for money. I don't know if he thinks I understood this is what he wanted all along, but—feeling I have been tricked—I decline and climb into the vehicle.

From the school we drive to today's destination—Tarangire, the fourth largest national park in Tanzania. Located south of the Maasailand plains, southeast of Lake Manyara and a three-hour's drive from Arusha, Tarangire has only about 20% of the number of annual visitors as the Serengeti.

The 1600 square mile park is named for the Tarangire River that meanders through it, providing a permanent source of water. During the dry season (roughly August-October), the river draws a concentration of animals that is second only to Ngorongoro Crater. In contrast to the migration in the Serengeti, which moves in a clockwise circle, in Tarangire it is an expansion and contraction. In the dry season, migratory animals move into the park, leaving again when the rains come. Increasing agriculture around the park's perimeter poses a serious potential threat to this migration pattern.

The Tarangire landscape lacks the dramatic volcanic evidence of prehistoric tectonic shifts that dominate the parks in the Great Rift

Valley area. However, the giant old baobabs that dot the rolling acacia woodlands in the most heavily used part of Tarangire have a drama of their own. The baobabs are sometimes called "upside down trees" because their massive trunks end in a wild tangle of squiggly branches resembling roots. One of the most breathtaking sights in Tanzania is a single colossal baobab backlit by the fiery red and orange of the setting sun. Add an elephant silhouette or two at the base of the tree and you have the image most commonly used to represent Tarangire.

Elephants are the main event in the park. Families of females and babies come together to form herds that can number in the hundreds. Herds of massive bulls can also be spotted; although these groups are fewer in number of members, the awesome size of the individual animals can make them equally impressive. Many of the baobabs in the park show signs of elephant abuse; in extremely dry times the animals strip the flesh of the trees for their high water content. The larger trees can withstand such rough treatment to a degree, making the baobab a renewable resource. Tanzanians use the fibrous wood to make woven mats and ropes.

Over time, some of the older trees have become hollowed out so that rainwater collects inside. The hollow spaces have also been used for shelter. Perhaps the most famous of Tarangire's baobabs is Poacher's Baobab, which has a diameter of 10 meters and is estimated to be over 3000 years old. There is a small opening in the side of the tree, which leads to a cavernous open interior roomy enough for as many as 20 people. The space must have a thousand stories to tell.

On my third safari we stopped at a large hollow baobab in Tarangire for a photo opportunity. As we walked up to the tree, a guide named Singo called out for us to wait until he had checked to make sure there wasn't a lion hiding inside. When we laughed at the idea, he told us of an experience he had several years earlier.

When he had pulled into an area with toilet facilities, a vehicle from another safari company was already there. The other driver shouted at Singo not to let his clients out of the Land Rover because there was a lion in the men's room. At first Singo thought his colleague was teasing him but it turned out to be true. When the other driver had arrived with his passengers, he was the first to reach the men's room. He opened the door to enter, saw the lion and had the presence of the mind—and the quick reflexes—to quickly shut it again. Everyone stayed in their vehicles until a park employee arrived on the scene, climbed up onto the roof of the men's room and reached down to open the door with a snare like device on a long pole. The lion—a big guy with a full mane—bolted out and disappeared into the distance, obviously not pleased to have been locked in the wash room.

After surveying the interior of the men's room, the park employee and the two drivers came up with an explanation for what had happened. Apparently the men's room door had been left open and the lion had gone in, probably seeking a relatively cool shady place to nap. The sink in the room had been torn from the wall and the mirror above it shattered. The guess was that the lion, seeing his reflection and thinking it was another lion, had lunged at the mirror and caused the destruction—and that the force of the animal's hitting the wall had caused the door to swing shut. It is a uniquely African story.

Our morning drive through Tarangire's baobab studded landscape ends at our lodge, a permanent tented camp perched on a hillside overlooking the river. The path from the main lodge to the sleeping tents has a sweeping view of the river valley below. As I follow the staff person carrying my duffle, I watch a big elephant walking in the water.

My platform tent has a deck-like front porch with a table and chairs—and that same great view of the river below. The tent itself is divided into two spaces. In the front is a spacious canvas sleeping area with two single cots, a table, a small wardrobe type of closet and large flaps that can be unzipped to let the breeze flow through. Through the back flap is a bathroom with cement floor, toilet, sink, shower, and concrete block walls that rise to about neck high, leaving an opening of several feet between the walls and the thatched roof. Each space has a bare light bulb that is powered by a generator for a few hours in the morning and evening.

After settling in, I walk back up the path to the main lodge for lunch. The outside wall of the large dining room is a screen so we feel as though we are eating in the open air. All the meals at Tarangire are buffets with a wide assortment of foods. As has been the case throughout our trip, the soup is especially remarkable. Encouraged by my success speaking Swahili at the school, I stop a waiter and ask,

*"Unasemaje 'soup' kwa Kiswahili?"* ("How do you say 'soup' in Swahili?")

He gives me a strange look, making think I have committed some terrible verbal blunder. Then he replies, "Soup."

I decide I want to hang out in this beautiful spot rather than going on the afternoon game drive. At the bar, I buy an icy cold Coca Cola in a glass bottle and take it to the roomy curved flagstone veranda in front of the main lodge. The view of the river is even better here. The elephant has disappeared but there is a giraffe bending down to drink, its legs splayed awkwardly. This is the only time an adult giraffe is vulnerable to lions. When they are upright, their legs pack a powerful punch capable of killing a lion but the sprawled out stance they must adopt in order to drink removes that advantage. In this case, the giraffe safely satisfies his thirst and, moving back to an upright position, undulates away into the cover of the trees.

I visit the lodge gift shop, which is outstanding. There is a wide assortment of merchandise ranging from inexpensive souvenirs like key chains to pieces of folk art such as carvings and sculptures. I purchase several rayon versions of kangas. (Real kangas are cotton.) They are fringed and the designs are in muted batik, much subtler than the kangas I have seen. Back home I will use them as tablecloths.

When I walk back down the path to my tent, I encounter many vervet monkeys, including babies the size of kittens, doing acrobatics in the tree canopies and chasing each other up and down the trunks. They take no notice of my passing.

I spend the afternoon sitting on my front porch enjoying a soft breeze and writing postcards to friends and family. As it gets later, activity at the river increases making it more and more difficult to concentrate on anything else. A large herd of zebra comes to drink, their shrill barking carrying clearly to where I am sitting. This is the sound I come to associate most strongly with Tanzania.

Several large birds perform an air ballet over the river valley. They are Bateleur eagles, their black, brown and chestnut feathers rippling as they swoop and glide. Near the path I see several types of smaller birds, including tiny multi-colored bee-eaters, barbets and bright lime green lovebirds.

A big baboon troop comes up the hillside from the river toward camp, their screeching becoming louder as they get closer to me. I watch as the baboons move across the path and disappear behind our tents. When I go inside to use the toilet, I first have to fish out a vividly colored frog. I wonder what else might come in through the gap above the bathroom walls. Then I look up at the thatched roof and speculate on what might live in it.

I had thought I was the only person who stayed behind this afternoon but I see Terry, a high school teacher from Wisconsin, walking laps back and forth on the path. He did the same thing on the Serengeti but there is more room here to stretch his legs. I admire his discipline but choose to continue my lazy lounging.

At dinner I learn some other members of our group had spent the afternoon at the swimming pool. Teenager Jenna tells us the water was very cold and the water slide was slow. We adults are less critical—we think it is amazing that we are staying at a lodge in the African bush that has a swimming pool. As Jenna's dad Skip observes, this is definitely "luxurious roughing it."

I get back to my tent before the generator goes off so I turn on the light when I go into the bathroom to wash my face. It immediately attracts a thick cloud of flying insects, one of which looks to be the "Godzilla" of the bug world. I quickly retreat to the forward part of my tent and cross my fingers that I won't need the bathroom in the middle of the night.

# Kumi (10)

It is Tuesday, the day of the week several people in the group are scheduled to take their dreaded weekly dose of Larium. This malaria medication causes a number of side effects, including nightmares. My doctor did not prescribe it for me; instead I am taking the antibiotic Doxycycline. Unfortunately, "doxy" increases sensitivity to the sun, which is somewhat problematic if your destination is near the Equator. My arms and hands have developed a strange rash and are swollen.

Skip, who is a physician, tells me it looks like sun poisoning. I have been using sunscreen with a heavy duty SPF but apparently that has not been enough. Today I keep a long sleeved shirt on throughout the game drive. (I took Doxycycline again in 2001 but in 2004, I switched to Malarone, which worked very well for me with no noticeable side effects.)

We see elephants, elephants and more elephants. I have been to Tarangire three times and the elephant sightings in the park have always been outstanding. Today we spend a long time observing a very large group cross a riverbed. Every time we think, "Okay, looks like that's the last one", another emerges from the trees—and another and another. There are elephants of all ages and all sizes, many of them more brown than gray from the cooling dust baths the animals take to protect their skin from the sun.

The Swahili name for elephant is *"Tembo"*. Weighing up to six tons or more, elephants are the largest living land mammals—the last surviving remnants of numerous massive mammals that roamed the earth in prehistoric times. In addition to their size, elephants have several other distinctive features. The first is their versatile trunk, which is definitely a multi-tasking tool. It is used for grabbing, digging, drinking, communicating, spraying and many other functions. The trunk is capable of both gentle, delicately controlled movements and feats of brute strength.

Tusks are another distinctive elephant feature; in African elephants, both males and females have tusks. Just as humans are right or left handed, elephants have a favored tusk that, because it is used more, is shorter than the other. Each elephant's tusks are unique, becoming more so with age. Along with ears, tusks are used by researchers to identify individual elephants. Tusks are teeth—dramatically elongated incisors - that continue to grow throughout an elephant's life. Today, the heaviest tusks probably weigh no more than 100 pounds compared to over 200 before poaching claimed the lives of the biggest elephants in Africa. Because it is an inherited characteristic, removing those elephants from the reproducing population has had a permanent impact on tusk size.

Large ears are so associated with elephants that people with big ears are often teased by being called "Dumbo". The ears of African elephants are significantly larger than those of their Asian counterparts. Elephants can reduce their body temperature by almost ten degrees by flapping their ears because they contain so many surface blood vessels.

The structure of an elephant's foot deadens sound, allowing it to move silently. That can infuse an eerie quality into an elephant watching experience. You expect something that big to thump when it walks but elephants sometimes appear to be gliding on a cushion of air. When we were observing that huge group cross the riverbed, I had a sense that someone had pushed the "mute" button. There was this mind-boggling amount of tonnage moving down one bank and up the next but the earth didn't shake and there was no sound of thundering hooves.

It is impossible to spend much time around elephants without being struck by their intelligence and their deep feeling for one another. On his website, Jeffrey Masson, co-author with Susan McCarthy of *"When Elephants Weep"* quotes scientist Douglas Chadwick, "If I learned anything from my time among the elephants it is the extent to which we are kin. The warmth of their families makes me feel warm. Their capacity for delight gives me joy. Their ability to learn and understand things is a continuing revelation for me. If a person can't see these qualities when looking at elephants, it can only be because he or she doesn't want to."

In addition to elephants, the morning's other sightings include a small monitor lizard swimming in a crystal creek, giraffe, wildebeest, baboons, impala, and more of the shy, big-eyed dik-dik. We spot an oryx for the first time. Unlike most antelope, the horns on an oryx are not curved but rather straight and spear like; they are ringed and can be as long at 30 inches.

We also see a saddle-billed stork searching for grasshoppers along the shoreline of a creek. This bird is an explosion of color—black, white, red and yellow. It looks like something from a Disney cartoon. One of Africa's largest storks, the saddle-bill has the graceful, slow motion walk typical of its species. The "saddle" is a yellow band across the bill. The birds have red knees and feet and some have a red spot or "medal" on their black chests. Saddle-bills put on a very entertaining show when they fish. The bird stretches out its long neck, grabs the fish in a lightening fast move and snaps the spine with its beak. It then swishes the fish in the water to wash it, tosses it up in the air and swallows it headfirst.

We follow a beautiful male lion in his prime for a quite a while. I think we all get some great photos. The poor lion just wants to take a nap; he finally hides in some bushes. With nothing more to see, we leave him to his peace and quiet.

Ruth gives two talks after lunch—one on baobabs and the other on hyena. Most of us are surprised to discover that, contrary to popular opinion, hyenas are not solely scavengers. They are actually more successful hunters than lions—and it is the latter that steal hyena kills rather than the other way around. Hyenas are the victims of some seriously bad press. Although they have the reputation of being cowardly, timid and sneaky, they actually are brave bold animals that are dangerous to both wildlife and humans.

The hyena is Africa's most common large carnivore; it is an opportunistic feeder, going for the easiest and most appealing food. If there is plenty of fresh prey available, hyena will pass up carrion but if the latter is all they can find, they can live on it. They will also eat vegetation and there are stories of them consuming aluminum pots from campsites. When a pack of hyena finishes feeding, there are few leftovers; they eat everything including skin and bones. Anything they can't digest is regurgitated in the form of pellets.

The position of a hyena's tail is helpful in reading the animal's moods. The *Wild Lives Guidebook* says, "When a hyena's tail is carried straight, for example, it signals attack. When it is held up and forward over the back, the hyena is extremely excited. In contrast, it hangs down when the hyena is standing or walking leisurely. If frightened, the hyena tucks its tail between the legs and flat against the belly and usually skulks away."

When I return to my tent after Ruth's talks, I learn I have just missed an elephant on the other side of the path. By the time I arrive on the scene, he is moving down the slope toward the river. I snap a picture of his rear end leaning lazily against a tree.

Deciding to skip the afternoon game drive again, I take a nap. I am so tired that the barking of zebra at the river and the noise of people moving back and forth along the path don't faze me—I sleep for an hour and a half. When I wake, I discover that I have missed out on more excitement. While he was sitting on his porch reading, Lynn looked up and saw the elephant had moved back toward the tents and was munching vegetation about 50 yards away.

Soon after, the big gray beast ambled up to the bathroom behind Ed and Betty's tent and began to scratch its side against the corner of the structure—while Betty was in the shower! To add insult to injury, later in the afternoon, Betty found a snake in the laundry basket.

In spite of the fact that it is possible for critters to get into the bathroom area, this tented camp remains one of my favorite places to stay in Tanzania. However in 2004, my safari used another Tarangire permanent tented camp called Kikoti. Located on the outer edge of the park (which meant limited walking safaris and night drives were permitted), it was a wonderful facility. The lodging was divided into sleeping and bathroom spaces but it was a huge, two room tent so there were no gaps through which invited visitors could enter. Solar power provided electricity 24 hours a day.

The tents, which were far apart and somewhat isolated from one another, were elevated; several steps led up to a spacious deck. This provided both a view over the tall grass that covered the site and also some protection from animals. Marked sandy paths through the tall grass connected the tents to the main lodge, which was a huge open covered space with wooden decking.

A number of Maasai were employed at Kikoti as *"askari"* or "watchmen"; carrying rifles, they escorted us between the tents and the main lodge after dark. On the morning after we arrived, I understood why that was necessary. As I walked to breakfast, I saw fresh lion prints in the soft sand of the path in front of my tent. In addition, we had all heard hyenas in the camp during the night.

One night at Kikoti, the evening meal was served outside - in an area enclosed by a thick thorn tree fence. The Maasai staff put on an extraordinary dance performance for us before dinner. By that time, I had seen a number of Maasai performances at various bomas during the daytime; but this was a totally different experience.

The deep darkness was pierced only by a campfire and a few flickering candles on the tables. The setting was timeless; there was nothing visible that placed us at the threshold of the 21st century. In the firelight, the dancers' red robes glowed like embers and the reflections off their spears, jewelry and bright teeth made it appear that sparks were shooting from their bodies. Each time a Maasai stepped forward from the line to jump, he was joined by his shadow twin.

The men's low pulsating chant grew louder as they danced. We joined our voices with theirs until the entire area was throbbing with a visceral roar that seemed to be coming directly from the center of the earth. We were glad when the Maasai pulled us into the dance with them. We felt an almost physical desire to be part of the ritual.

When the performance ended and I returned winded to my chair, I felt like I had been released from some kind of possession. I thought about what it must have been like for early white explorers to come to Africa and encounter such a spectacle not as entertainment but in a setting of aggression. The Maasai have a reputation for being fierce warriors; I could see how rites such as this one could serve to whip them into a frenzy that would make them feel invincible.

Glad as I am to have experienced Kikoti, if I had to choose I think I prefer this camp above the river valley where we stayed on my first trip. Today, when everyone is back from the afternoon game drive, we come together to meet Charles and Laura Foley from the Tarangire Elephant Project. They speak to us about the work they have been doing for the past decade. We learn male elephants have rounded foreheads and that the heads of older bulls sometimes take on an hourglass shape. The heads of female elephants are more pointed. The bellies of bulls slope up toward the front, while female bellies are flat across because their breasts are located between their front legs.

The oldest, biggest female leads elephant families or "cow herds". When the group exceeds about ten individuals, they usually split, although the resulting separate families often stay in close proximity and interact frequently. When they reach puberty at about 12 years of age, males leave the cow herds and join bachelor groups or wander alone. By twenty-five, bulls are usually large enough to begin to compete for reproductive rights. Foley tells us that the musk smell of a colossal old bull in search of a female in estrus is one of the strongest odors on earth.

Not all of the information is that innocuous. We also hear that high levels of poaching, which resulted when people turned to ivory for investment purposes after OPEC was formed took the lives of hundreds of thousands of African elephants. Because the poachers were looking for the largest tusks, they first killed the big males and then the oldest of the matriarchs in families. To this day, clans that did not retain sufficient numbers of older females continue to suffer even though the ivory ban has been in place for years.

Elephants must survive natural cycles that span decades. If a family does not have any matriarchs old enough to remember how the clan dealt with a crisis that last occurred several decades earlier, they don't know what to do or where to go to survive it when it recurs. The families with older matriarchs know to leave the park and go to the mountains in times of severe drought. Herds without those resources remain and suffer horribly, especially the babies.

Tanzania continues to be adamantly opposed to lifting of the ivory ban—even to allow the sale of ivory amassed by governments from elephants that have died natural deaths. The country's position is that it will be too difficult to prevent a black market in illicit ivory if sales of any kind are sanctioned. That is a pretty courageous stance for a country as poor as Tanzania.

After so many excellent meals, I decide to skip dinner; I go back to my tent, have a nutrition bar and turn in early. During the night, I am awakened several times by animal noises, including once by lion roars that sound very close.

# Kumi Na Moja (11)

So far, our Tarangire excursions have been limited to the acacia and baobab-covered woodlands. Today, we venture to the distant, and seldom visited, environs of the Silale swamp and wetlands. This is not a drive you want to take in the wet season. The "black cotton" soil—so named because it is ideal for growing cotton—absorbs huge amounts of water and becomes a thick, sucking, and impassable mire. In contrast, during the dry season, it can develop cracks ten feet deep.

On the drive to the Silale, we enjoy an up-close encounter with an elephant family. Last night's talk gives us more understanding of the interactions we see. We know the matriarchs will not tolerate for much longer the unruly antics of the adolescent males who are wrestling and disturbing the peace. Soon they will be pushed out of the family; they will wander alone or in small groups for years until they are massive enough to become one of the giant bulls that enjoy breeding rights.

We are too noisy for one big female. She goes through various aggressive posturing designed to put us on notice. We know from what the Foleys said—and from the driver's reassurance—that we are in no danger. Even so, her challenging behavior is unnerving. Skip writes in the group journal, "I was very familiar with her moves, having been personally confronted with an elephant last night while I was on foot outside the pool. She even took a couple of steps as a bluff charge, complete with trumpeting! Not something likely to happen in Maine."

Over 300 varieties of birds have been recorded in Tarangire and we see many of them today—plovers, weavers, lovebirds, bee-eaters, kori bustard, ostrich, rollers, vultures, ibis, go-away birds, shrikes, southern ground hornbills and more. We also spot the hamerkop, a bird known for building enormous, multi-chambered nests—a new one each year. As we get closer to the swamplands, we see a growing number of water birds - egrets, Egyptian ducks, saddle-billed storks, yellow-billed storks, and fish eagles. In one area we spot a very large group of pelicans.

We are the only safari vehicles in the swamp and we happen on one of the most extraordinary sightings of our entire safari. A very large lion pride has a Cape buffalo kill in the water. When we arrive, females and a young male are feeding. Shortly thereafter, one of the pride's dominant males, his belly grossly distended from what he has already eaten, waddles out into the water and chases the females away. He tolerates the young male briefly but then there is a skirmish accompanied by growling, splashing, and much showing of teeth; the younger lion retreats onto the grass.

The young male and some of the females occasionally venture tentatively out toward the kill but the dominant male keeps them at bay. He wrestles with the carcass, trying to shift it to get to the uneaten portion under the water line.

A number of females and cubs of various ages are lying in the grassy area around the water. We catch a brief glimpse of some babies but two females quickly lead them from our view. After an hour or so, we shift our location, driving away from the water to where a second male and several females are sleeping. When we get there, we see this is where the tiny cubs have been taken. The lions are so sated from their big meal that they don't even bother to move the babies again so we get to watch them cavort and tumble. Occasionally, they try to engage one of the sleeping adults, all of which ignore them. They have to be content with one another's company.

The male in this area looks much older than the one in the water and he does not appear to be in good health. The younger one is wise to be building up his strength because his partner will not be much help if their coalition's control of the pride is challenged by outsiders.

Once the novelty of watching the lions begins to wear off a bit, we look around and realize there is a great deal more to see. In addition to the many birds that are sprinkled along the shoreline and in the grass, we see elephants and zebra in the distance. We think the elephants might be a clan that Charles Foley had mentioned last night, a dysfunctional group with no older matriarchs that hides out in the swamp much of the time.

The only Cape buffalo we see today is the one the lions had killed; and we have only seen individuals and small groups previously. However, huge herds of buffalo have been reported in Tarangire. In the wet season, groups of over 1000 have been seen. Given the foul temperament of the animal, I am not sure I would want to run into hundreds of them in one place.

Prior to going to Tanzania, I was under the mistaken assumption that the African, or Cape buffalo was the same as the water buffalo, a domesticated animal found in many parts of the world. The two animals are similar in appearance but the Cape is wild and more dangerous.

Known as *"Nyati"* in Swahili, the Cape buffalo is one of the African "Big Five"—the other four being lion, elephant, leopard and rhino. Although Cape buffalo resemble cattle, they are much more unpredictable—placid much of the time but vicious if cornered or wounded.

Both female and male African buffalo have distinctive curved horns, which are powerful weapons against predators. When attacked, herds form an outward facing circle around the young so that their horns form a hard to penetrate defense. Although the primary purpose of this behavior is to protect the young, it also benefits impaired adult members of the herd. When lions are successful in killing a buffalo it usually is an older solitary male. If a buffalo calf is separated from the herd and in danger, it bellows loudly and the adults come to its rescue.

Cape buffalo can weigh up to 1500 pounds. The animals have a keen sense of smell but relatively poor hearing and eyesight. They graze mostly at night, spending the day hanging out in the shade or wallowing in the cool mud. Clashes with the interests of the human population—they raid crops and spread disease to livestock—have diminished Cape buffalo numbers.

We spend so long watching the lion pride with their kill that we get back to the lodge just before they stop serving lunch, which is Mexican food, African style. As we eat, we watch a very large baboon meander along the top of the low wall surrounding the veranda outside the dining room. A woman is sitting in the middle of the veranda near the wall, facing the opposite direction from the baboon. She is so startled when he passes into her field of vision, that she jumps straight up and shrieks, frightening the animal and causing him to almost leap out of his skin. As he continues on his way, he glances back at her a couple of times, the look on his face saying, "What is wrong with you, Lady?" Later, the baboon returns, bringing a number of his buddies. If he is looking to "rumble" with the woman who had frightened him, she is long gone.

Because we stayed out so long this morning, the afternoon game drive will be a short one; a number of us stay in camp. I join Ruth and Terry in walking a few laps back in front of the lines of tents on each side of the main lodge. It is a warm, sunny day and the location of the camp makes it seem like we are perched on top of the world. There is a huge expanse of sky above us and down below the Tarangire River wiggles and winds through the valley.

We watch a family of elephants that comes to drink and hang out by the water. A couple of youngsters spar with their trunks, their mock fighting a way to develop and hone skills they will use for the rest of their lives. We also see giraffe, zebra and a beautiful male waterbuck, whose antlers look impressive even from this distance. Waterbuck have a longish sumptuous coat and big velvet eyes. I think their faces are the most beautiful of all the antelope. The animal also has distinctive white markings on its rump.

Once again, the sky fills with large birds as the day begins to fade. They ride the warm air currents and use their sharp eyes to search for dinner in the river valley beneath them. We are enjoying a particularly beautiful sunset when the afternoon game drive returns. They report a leopard sighting but I have no regrets about having stayed behind

Dinner is a cookout. Afterwards, we sit in the outdoor bar and enjoy the evening. We drink Tusker beer and African wine and re-live our last game drive day. Tomorrow we head to Zanzibar for the final phase of our trip. Now that we are closer to the end than to the beginning of our adventures our talk more and more often turns to home. We are missing family, friends and pets.

# Kumi Na Mbili (12)

I was mistaken in thinking that yesterday would be the pinnacle of our game viewing; this morning's experience tops it. When I unzip my tent flap and step out onto the porch, there is a large elephant right on the other side of the path—maybe 40 feet away. After the initial shock, I see there is a small family of about ten individuals, including the tiniest baby we have yet seen, scattered along the path between my tent and the main lodge.

It is a little nerve wracking to walk to breakfast past so many elephants in such close proximity. I wave at Jim and Lloryn who later tell me they had been sitting on their porch since first light quietly watching the elephants wander among the trees, grazing peacefully. We could not have asked for a more fabulous conclusion to our time in the bush.

We drive to the Arusha Hotel and from there walk across the parking circle to nearby shops. There have been a number of opportunities to shop so far on the trip—at lodges, at the Maasai boma and along the road. Just about every time we have stopped somewhere outside of the parks, vendors have emerged from nowhere to offer all kinds of merchandise for sale. The entrepreneurial spirit is alive and well in Tanzania.

I have pretty much completed my shopping list. However, some members of our group are still looking for some things to take back as gifts or souvenirs. I poke my head in a couple of shops, looking specifically for Heidi Lange batiks but have no luck. Sometimes I step into a store just to get away from the aggressive street vendors. On the sidewalk progress is slow going because there are so many of them and they will not take "no" for an answer. (I do find that saying "no" in Swahili—"*hapana*"—is somewhat more effective.) After a bit, I give up and walk back over to the Arusha and browse in its gift shop there while I wait for the rest of the group to return.

Lunch is at the Impala Hotel where we spent our first night in Africa. The drivers, who normally eat separately, are our guests because this is the last time we will see them. After the meal, we make a presentation to each of them—the poetry and jokes and singing hiding deep emotion. We have grown to care for these four wonderful young men and we are regretful to part with them. Over the past couple of days, a tip envelope has been circulated and a committee appointed by Ruth has divided the money collected into four sealed envelopes. After giving the envelopes to the drivers, there are some last hugs and photographs before we leave to catch our flight to Zanzibar.

I have read different explanations of the origin of the name "Zanzibar". Some of the Persian or Arabic words that have been credited include *zangh* ("Negro") and *bar* ("coast"), *zinj el barr* ("land of the blacks") and *zayn za'l barr* (fair is this island). At one time "Zanzibar" was used to denote both the archipelago made up of Zanzibar and Pemba islands and the adjacent coast. Zanzibar Island's Swahili name is *Unguja*.

"Swahili", which comes from the Arabic word "*sahil*", meaning "of the coast," began in Zanzibar as a language of commerce. During the 18th and 19th centuries caravans traveling the great trade routes spread Swahili throughout Eastern and into Central Africa. Swahili is a second language for most Tanzanians, the first being their tribal language.

Originally, we were scheduled to fly to Zanzibar out of Arusha but the flight has been cancelled so the drivers take us to the Kilimanjaro airport, leaving us where we had first met them 12 days earlier. The plane is late but once we are boarded, the flight is uneventful. Landing in Zanzibar, we experience the ambivalent relationship the island has with the mainland. We are required to go through Customs and have our passports stamped even though we have not left Tanzania.

As soon as we step off the plane, we wilt in the extreme heat and humidity. We are very pleased when our tour operator escorts us to an air-conditioned bus for the ride to the Serena Inn in Zanzibar Town on the western side of the island. When we arrive, we are greeted by a turbaned doorman who is wearing an elaborately embroidered vest over his white shirt and pants. He ushers us into an opulent lobby full of ornate carved wood trim. As we have come to expect, wet cloths and fresh squeezed juice await us.

Unfortunately, there has been a mistake in the reservations and Pat and I have to share a room. The hotel is totally booked for the night but the manager Alex promises to try to give us single accommodations the next day. Our room is marvelous, with beds swathed in mosquito netting, a balcony, a luxurious bathroom—and air conditioning.

The hotel is located right on the Indian Ocean and is oriented in such a way that a refreshing breeze sweeps through the hallways. As long as we stay out of the direct sun when we are outside, we are quite comfortable. Standing by the sensational swimming pool, surrounded by lavish landscaping and looking out over the breathtaking blue-green waters of the ocean as dhows sail by in the distance, I almost pinch myself to see if I am dreaming. After thinking about it, I decide that—if I am—it's a great dream and I don't want to wake up.

The restaurant extends over the edge of the water and at dinner we hear the waves splashing on the rocks below. The fragrance of saltwater and exotic flowers wafts in through the open windows by our tables. An additional breeze from the ceiling fans above us—which are spinning faster than I would have thought possible—helps to keep us cool.

Each of our place settings has more silverware than any of us has ever seen. After we order, the staff glides around the table, removing some pieces and adding others, depending on whether our entrée is fowl, meat or fish. It all speaks to the privileged lives of early white colonists and wealthy expatriates—a lifestyle with which none of us is familiar. When our food arrives, we consult on which fork to use and dig in. My pasta salsa appetizer and beef medallions are sublime. Dessert is a mango jellyroll served on vanilla and chocolate sauce. I think perhaps this is the life I am meant to live.

# Kumi Na Tatu (13)

It is 8:20 in the morning and I am sitting on a terrace at the hotel looking out over the Indian Ocean, my journal lying forgotten in my lap. It is already much warmer and stickier than just an hour ago when I had breakfast. The meal was a buffet; I passed on the oxtail soup but did try the hibiscus jam, which tasted as flowery as its name.

At dinner last night it was too dark to see that there are stained glass skylights in the restaurant ceiling—the colors rich and beautiful but even so, no competition for those of the ocean. The water seems striped, light and translucent at the shoreline and progressing in bands of deepening combinations of green and blue until it becomes an inky black on the horizon.

A small boat goes by in front of me. It is overfilled with six or seven men, two of them bailing as fast as they can with plastic containers. None of the men appears concerned that their craft is taking on water. Perhaps the situation is not as dire as it seems to me; they are still afloat when they disappear from sight.

At 8:30 we board our mini-bus and drive through scenes that look and feel very different from the mainland. Jim writes in the group journal, "We hurl ourselves through narrow streets, past markets with tropical fruits and scores of bicycles, past pickup truck buses with people and produce hanging from every nook and cranny. The people too are different and exotic. The Arab and Islamic influence permeates the atmosphere and you might be in Casablanca."

By 10 a.m. we are at the Jozani Forest, home to the Zanzibar red colobus monkey, also known as Kirks Red Colobus. Numbering only about 1500, they are one of Africa's most rare primates. A Swahili name for the red colobus is *kima punju* or "poison monkey." Local folklore associates the monkeys with a poison that causes crops and trees to die and dogs to lose their hair.

It has started to rain so we have our umbrellas up, making it virtually impossible to take photographs of the monkeys in the thick branches overhead. There are so many of them moving about it is as though the trees are alive, their leaves shivering in the rain.

The colobus are circus performers, trapeze artists without nets. They tumble and swing, leap and twist, sometimes using one another as ropes to get to the next branch. They peer down at us through the leaves, their mouths stretched in what look like smiles of pleasure at our company.

There are many young romping with wild abandon like kindergarteners on a playground jungle gym. We also see tiny babies, clinging shyly to their mothers. The trees have fat green waxy leaves, the undersides of which are the same red brown as the fur on the monkeys' backs. Sometimes we think we are seeing a colobus when really the monkey has come and gone, its movement leaving behind a quivering leaf that catches our attention.

The rain stops as we walk back to the reception area where a guide with a lilting accent and a colorful vocabulary tells us Jozani is a conservation area that preserves some of the last indigenous forest left on Zanzibar. As the guide leads us on a walk through the forest, the humidity is so high that we are quickly soaked to the skin. When it starts to rain again, we figure we cannot get any wetter so we do not bother with the umbrellas. The guide entertains us with a running narrative of how natives use the trees and plants we pass for medicines and "witch doctoring." Our visit concludes with a stroll along wooden decks through a mangrove swamp. In the mud and water by the trees' roots, we can see many tiny crabs.

When we return to the hotel—with wet clothes and stringy hair—Alex greets me with the key to my new room. It is the Honeymoon Suite situated on a corner of the roof. It has a king sized bed covered in crisp white linens and piled with plump pillows. The mosquito netting is voluminous and so gossamer fine it might have been spun by spiders. Sunlight streams in from French doors leading to a wraparound deck with an oversized hammock in a hand carved wooden stand. Of course, there is a view of the ocean!

Later in the evening when I am dressing for dinner, musicians in white robes set up in the area under the balcony and begin to play. From my vantage point, it feels like a private performance expressly for my benefit—although I know they actually are entertaining people sitting in an adjacent patio bar.

After lunch, several of us go in search of local shops in the area around the hotel. Once we leave the upscale Serena beachfront property and enter the nearby narrow twisting streets, we are in a different world. The buildings are very old and many are dilapidated but their style is beguiling and whispers of bygone glory days. We glimpse a bit of latticework here, a curved iron stairway there, the suggestion of a courtyard hidden just beyond crumbling walls—and we see many examples of the handsome, carved and brass studded doors for which the island is famous.

After exploring a few small shops, we find one called "Zanzibar Memories" that is a treasure trove of merchandise—tanzanite and silver jewelry, clothing, leatherwork, rugs, batiks (including Heidi Lange), wall hangings, carvings and more. As we walk back to the hotel with our purchases, we pass silent men—we see no women on the streets - who seem to observe us intently but who do not acknowledge us in any way. Even though the women in our group are dressed in respect for local custom—no shorts or sleeveless tops, nothing transparent—I feel we are being judged and found lacking. I know tourist dollars are important to the island and its people but I do not get the sense that our being there and spending our money endears us to the men we pass.

The men live in a Zanzibar we do not see. The Zanzibar Poverty Reduction Plan (ZPRP), which has as its objective improved living conditions for all Zanzibaris, refers to statistics from a Household Budget Survey that cites illiteracy rates of 40% on the island overall and 60% for women. Life expectancy is less than 50 years and the average annual income per person is only US$137. The statistics are dated but there is no reason to believe things have significantly improved since they were gathered—and some conditions may be worse.

Back in the insulated environment of the Serena, we show off our purchases, some of us wearing our new kangas as skirts to dinner. This is our last night in Africa. We came together as strangers only two weeks ago but the experiences we have shared make it seem we have known each other for much longer. Tonight we raise our glasses in a toast that includes both sadness and anticipation. We know that after we say farewell tomorrow most of us will never meet again. However, we also know tomorrow will take us home

# Kumi Na Nne (14)

It is almost midnight and my flight to Amsterdam has just taken off from the Dar es Salaam airport. Two weeks and four hours after arriving in Tanzania, I am on the way back home.

This morning we went to Stone Town, which is sometimes called the "heart of Zanzibar." Stone Town is very much as it was two centuries ago and it has the distinction of being the only still functioning historic town in East Africa. The *"Spectrum Guide to Tanzania"* includes an 1879 quote about Stone Town from Captain James Frederic Elton, a former British Vice-Consul for Zanzibar, "An architectural background of Arabian arches, heavy carved wooden doors and lintel posts, circular towers, narrow latticed windows, recesses and raised terraces, combined with and worked into tortuous lanes and sharp turnings, wells in unexpected corners, squalor, whitewash, dirt and evil smells as you penetrate further into the heart of the town." Over 100 years later, Elton would have no trouble recognizing Zanzibar.

Our first stop was a sprawling open market, offering wares ranging from kangas to live pigs being slaughtered on the spot. One stall was selling chickens—missing their heads but with feet still attached - that were being prepared for purchase by having their feathers plucked and then being dunked, one after another, in a small bucket of dirty water.

After the market, we visited a building where slaves were once held in a dungeon-like basement until they were auctioned. By the 19th century, Zanzibar under Oman rule was the primary slave-trading depot in Africa. It is estimated that over one-half million slaves were sold through Zanzibar between 1830 and 1873 when a British treaty with the sultan closed down the island's slave trade.

I was so distressed by the sadness of the place's history that I could not go down into the basement. Later, I felt small for not being able to voluntarily face for a moment what so many people had been forced to endure for days—and then only as a prelude to something worse.

British Captain Elton described the slave auction area, "When you go at an early hour and look at the strings of men, old women and children sitting upon the ground in lots, and the rows of younger, better favoured and higher priced girls, bedecked for the occasion with heavy earrings and bangles and bright coloured robes—all the faces marked with the vacant stare common to the slave population—I protest the sight is a revolting one, and it is rendered doubly so when, as is often the case, some of the recently imported wretches are mere skeletons of skin and bone, festering with sores and loathsome skin-diseases, and looking as if they were on the very threshold of death."

Our next stop was Christ Church, which stands on the site of the old slave market. The clock that is the dominant feature on the outside of the church was donated by Sultan Sayyid Barghash; his stipulation in making the gift was that the height of the church could not be greater than that of his palace. Inside the church we saw things we had read about many times—the columns that were accidentally installed upside down, the altar located in the spot where slaves used to be whipped and the crucifix that is believed to have been made from the tree under which David Livingstone died.

In Dr. Livinstone's time, conditions in Zanzibar were so bad that he called the island, "the open sore of the world" and expressed the opinion it should be re-named "Stinkibar." Livingstone's harsh opinion of Zanzibar was rooted largely in his opposition to slavery. A letter Livingstone sent home describing the slaughter of villagers by slave traders on the Lualaba River so enraged his countrymen that it led to the British treaty that halted the Zanzibar slave trade. Of himself, Livingstone wrote, "I am a missionary, heart and soul. God had an only Son, and He was a missionary and a physician. A poor, poor imitation of Him I am, or wish to be. In this service I hope to live; in it I wish to die."

Livingstone got his wish; he was still working and serving in Africa when he died on April 30, 1872. After drying his body to preserve it, his two native assistants made a perilous 11-month journey to transport the body and Livingstone's papers the 1000 miles to Zanzibar. As he had requested, his heart was buried in Africa; his body was transported to England where it was buried in Westminster Abbey.

After the Stone Town tour, we returned to the hotel to get our luggage and then were driven to the airport for the short flight across the water to Dar es Salaam, capital of Tanzania and the departure city for our late night flight. The driver of the bus that picked us up when we landed gave us a mini-tour of Dar on the way to the hotel where we were having dinner. Apparently, Saturday is "wedding day" in the capital because we passed many wedding parties, particularly along the beach. One wedding procession was led by a pick up truck with a band playing in the back. The next truck contained the bride and groom. We leaned our heads out the windows of our bus to wave and shout our congratulations.

After driving by both the bombed out American Embassy and the new one that was under construction, we arrived at the hotel. We used shared "day rooms" to shower and change clothes and then gathered to break bread together one last time. At 9:00, Ruth escorted us to the bus and waved us off—she and Lynn were staying at the hotel overnight and continuing on to South Africa the next day.

The airport was hot and there were few amenities. As we waited for our flight to be called, we mostly sat in a kind of stupefied silence like we had just been returned to earth after an alien abduction. It was as though time had stopped for us for two weeks and now the clock was about to start ticking again. We would be on the same plane to Amsterdam and then we would go our separate ways, back to our separate realities.

For the moment, though, we were in a holding pattern, suspended between where we had been and where we were going. Already, we had lost our "groupness." When we lined up for boarding, it was as the individuals and couples we had been before we had met two weeks earlier.

Now, sitting in business class (thank goodness for frequent flyer miles) as the jet hurdles through space at 35,000 feet, my memories of the past two weeks seem almost too astounding to be real.

I have gazed upon the Ngorongoro Crater at twilight, I have greeted the dawn on the endless plains of the Serengeti, and I have watched the sun set over the Indian Ocean.

I have seen a lake of flamingos, a pool of hippos and a sea of wildebeest.

I have had banana stew, hibiscus jam and Tusker beer.

I have heard lions roar in the night, zebras bark at the river and musicians play in a truck.

I have been charged by an elephant, I have danced with the Maasai and I have drawn a bushman's bow.

I have been to Africa.

I close my eyes to try to get some rest on the long flight back. In my dreams, I see Tanzania.

# I See Tanzania

Specs of red on the hillside,
Impala locking horns,
Giraffe of awesome grace and calm
Nibbling on trees of thorns.

Zebras in the Crater mist
And running 'cross the plains;
Wildebeest streaming past our tents
As they follow the rains.

I see Tanzania.

Adolescent elephants
Mock fighting as they play,
Babies learning to use their trunks,
A bird named "Go Away".

Hippos floating on their backs
Their bellies fat and white;
Upside down trees called "Baobabs",
Warthogs spoiling for a fight.

I see Tanzania.

A mother of haunting beauty
Cradling her crippled boy.
Schoolchildren clothed in rags and dust
While singing songs of joy.

Gracious people working hard
To make things to our taste,
While feeding their own families
On less than what we waste.

I see Tanzania,

# EPILOGUE

For me, Tanzania was a case of love at first sight. It immediately began to speak to me in a language I did not even know I understood and I never want the conversation to end. I have been back twice since my first safari and I want to go again as soon as I am able. Ruth, who has become a good friend, says that I will be returning to Tanzania for the rest of my life and my heart tells me she is right.

I had never had a passport prior to my first safari. My travels outside the US had been limited to Mexico, Canada and the Bahamas—destinations for which my birth certificate was sufficient. When I announced I was returning to Tanzania a second—and then a third—time, the most common response was, "But you have already been there. You should go somewhere else."

Wow - only in America! Been there. Done that. Notch your belt and move on. People who return to the same beach house each summer, who buy a timeshare so they can go to Disney every year, who never tire of hunting at the same deer lease or visiting the mall—these people could not understand why I would want to travel more than once to the endless plains of the Serengeti, to the stirring expanse of the Great Rift Valley, to the lost world of the Ngorongoro Crater and to exotic Zanzibar.

It's not that I am uninterested in traveling to other places. I have never been to Paris or London or China or Spain. Australia sounds interesting and I love the idea of Tuscany. Then there is Costa Rica and Crete and Belize - the Galapagos, Antarctica, Tibet and Mongolia. If I had the time and the money to go on more than one big trip a year, these are some of the places I would explore. However, my circumstances force me to choose between "reach" and "depth". Rather than seeking a passing experience with many places, I prefer to cultivate a deep relationship with a single place I love.

What makes Tanzania so special? I have mentioned the warmth and graciousness of the people and hinted at the sense of safety I feel in the country. I had huge trepidations before my first trip; like many—if not most—Westerners, I visualized Africa as a place of high and constant danger. If the lions didn't get you, then the cannibals might. When I told my boss, a man of great wisdom and learning, that I was going on safari his response was, "Remember we are a small company—we can't afford a big ransom." He was half serious.

Tanzania is a very stable country without the inter-tribal conflict that is present in many parts of Africa. Julius Nyerere's vision of *ujamaa,* or "familyhood", is generally considered to have been an economic failure, but it helped to unify the country under his leadership. Tanzania is tolerant of religious and ethnic differences. It is a country of moderation and balance and it has the courage to act on what it values, even when sacrifice is required.

The first time I met Joseph Kitia, he said something I will always remember. "Tanzania is not a poor country but rather a country that has not yet fully developed its resources." One of Tanzania's underlying strengths is that it recognizes that its greatest resource is its people. Every Tanzanian I have asked to name the country's biggest challenge, top priority or most important opportunity has answered without hesitation, "Education." Men and women, wealthy and poor, literate and illiterate, urban and rural—virtually all Tanzanians share the same vision that education is the key to the country's future. I don't know of another nation in the world where you will find this kind of consistent focus.

In part at least, my love of Tanzania is rooted in selfishness. I like the person I am in Tanzania. My attempts to practice mindfulness in my day-to-day life here at home meet with only moderate success. I am always worrying about the next meeting, the next challenge, the next day. When I am in Tanzania, I don't have to try to be mindful; I am present in the moment without thinking about it. For me, Tanzania has a contagious serenity that centers me and slows me down. There is a harmony in Tanzania, a balance that seems to make life richer, at least for me.

In part, the difference has to do with "stuff". Except for missing my family, I am happier in Tanzania with a duffle and a camera bag than I am in the US with multiple cars, bedrooms, bathrooms, closets, and 90 pairs of shoes. I don't know why I can't—or don't—or won't—simply strip away some of the "stuff" that burdens my life here at home but so far I haven't.

Above and beyond all of this, I am in love with Tanzania because of its incredible natural beauty. This is one gorgeous place—and gorgeous in diverse ways. It has mountains and forests and hills and plains and beaches and islands and oceans and valleys and highlands and lakes and rivers. The trees seem taller, the foliage more lush, the flowers larger and more fragrant, the breezes softer, the ocean bluer, the mountains more majestic. The "Wow!" factor of the landscape is off the charts.

In the end my love affair with Tanzania is like all passion. It defies explanation and it requires none; it simply is what it is. It is a passion my family does not share; they have not accompanied me on any of my safaris. My husband Jim is not a traveler; he likes the routine of home. My twenty-something son James has a sense of adventure but it does not extend to Africa. When I have tried to bribe or cajole him into going with me, he has said, "Mom, that's your thing, not mine." My hope is for him to find a "thing" that brings him as much joy as my interest in Tanzania has brought to me.

In his Foreword to the *Wild Lives Guidebook,* African Wildlife Foundation Trustee John H. Heminway speaks for me when he writes, "'What have you, Africa, done to me? Why should I care that a fish eagle soars or elephants roll in mud or Maasai vanish into heat waves?' Your response: I must return."

I agree, too, with Heminway when he says, "I know all of this sounds a bit much, but if ever I have seen magic, it has been in Africa."

In Swahili, *safari* means "journey." Using that definition, each of us is on a safari everyday—what is life if not a journey? My road will take me back to Tanzania; wherever yours takes you, I wish you *safari njema*—a happy journey.

# APPENDIX A
## —Lessons I Learned in Africa

1. I am capable of being a morning person.

2. It can be liberating to give up control.

3. You don't have to speak their language to communicate with children.

4. Water is more valuable than diamonds

5. Silence can be healing.

6. Nature holds all the trump cards.

7. Sometimes civilized countries aren't.

8. Rich is relative.

9. Possessions own you.

10. Dust happens.

# APPENDIX B
# —Bibliography and Recommended Resources

Bechy, Allen, 1990, *Adventuring in East Africa,* Sierra Club Books

Benjamin, Mironko and Geoghegan, 2003, *Swahili Phrasebook,* Lonely Planet Publications

Briggs, Philip, *Tanzania the Bradt Travel Guide,* Bradt Publications

Fitzpatrick, Mary, *Tanzania Zanzibar and Pemba,* Lonely Planet Publications

Insight Guides, 1999, *East African Wildlife,* APA Publications

Masson, Jeffrey and McCarthy, Susan, 1995, *When Elephants Weep,* Dell Publishing

National Audubon Society, 1998, *Field Guide to African Wildlife,* Chanticleer Press

Reader, John, 1998, *A Biography of the Continent Africa,* First Vintage Books

Spectrum, 1998, *Guide to Tanzania,* Interlink Books

Trustees and Staff of African Wildlife Foundation, 1997, *Wild Lives Guidebook,* African Wildlife Foundation

*www.africantheart.com*

*www.awf.org*

*www.developmentgateway.org*

*www.earthwatch.org*

*www.egan.webstrikesolutions.com*

*www.goafrica.about.com*

*www.jeffreymasson.com*

*www.lionresearch.org*

*www.longelyplanet.com/destinations/africa/tanzania*

*www.maasai-infoline.com*

*www.sandiegozoo.org/animalbytes*

*www.serengeti.org*

*www.sierraclub.org/outings*

*www.tanzania.go.tz/profile.html*

*www.uniquesafaris.com*

*www.wildwatch.com/resources/birds*

*www.zanzibar-web.com*

Made in the USA
Lexington, KY
06 September 2014